Build Se
and Go It ...

ESCAPE CORPORATE W@NKERY

David –
keep paying it forward
– Phil Sterne
18-10-24

The guidance you need from someone who's done it.

PHIL STERNE

First published 2024.

In other words, the ideas contained within this book are based on my own experiences and my successes and failures. They may or may not work for you, and outcomes can vary.

Book cover by Phil Sterne and Joshua Frederick
Illustrations by Phil Sterne
Book interior design by Joshua Frederick

Edition 1, 2024
ISBN: 978-1-0686639-0-1

FOR:

NIC–YOU HELPED ME TAKE
THE BIGGEST OF STEPS

HOPE AND HARRISON–
GROW UP TO DO WHAT YOU LOVE

CONTENTS.

INTRODUCTION.

WHO IS THIS BOOK FOR?

You've had enough.

You've had enough of...
working all the hours to put money in someone else's pockets,
the micromanaging boss or toxic colleagues (or both),
the not being listened to (or heard),
the lack of opportunities to grow,
the being taken for granted,
the lack of recognition,
the lack of fulfilment,
the commute,
the bullshit,
or the pay.

Or something else I've not listed. It'll be personal to you. But these things have got on top of you, messed with your mind, and made you feel unhappy for too long.

Well, rest easy my friend. As Tom Jones would say, it's not unusual. Trust me, you are not the only one who feels like this. You hear people say "We're in the same boat", but I'd argue all the boats and all the treacherous waters differ in their capacity to drown us. It's our resolve, our mindset, and at times our bloody pluckiness that'll not only keep us afloat, but get us safely to the promised land.

You've spent years building your career, working for a manager (or if you're lucky, a leader) and going through the annual cycle, year after year. You may have switched jobs, moved companies, and even changed disciplines or sectors, each time learning new skills—job-specific and 'people' skills. What we used to call 'interpersonal skills'.

In fact, every day you have become microscopically better, more capable, and closer to operating in your 'Zone of Genius'[1] than the day before. But, like watching a tree grow, it's barely noticeable.

How many times have you met up with family or friends with kids you haven't seen in ages, and used those well-worn phrases that we always promised ourselves we wouldn't say? Phrases like "haven't you grown" and "I remember when you were *this* high". We say them for a reason.

At the time of writing, my son is 14 years old. Sometimes he can go to bed and get up in the morning looking an inch taller[2].

It's time that does this. The passage of time is an incredible thing and when we're left to our own devices, while no one is watching (not even ourselves), things are growing, evolving, and imperceptibly changing both in and all around us.

It's for this reason I believe that you more than likely won't know how good you really are. Others will see it. They might even tell you. But more often than not, you'll brush it off (particularly in the UK where we're terrible at receiving compliments) or just not believe what you're hearing. Or perhaps it just doesn't happen regularly enough to make much of an impact.

A bit like a light snowfall, there's never quite enough of it coming to settle properly, so it just sits and quietly melts away.

---

1 Psychologist and author in the field of personal growth, Gay Hendricks, coined the term 'Zone of Genius' to describe the point where you find yourself using your natural abilities and feeling joy and fulfilment. Others have referred to working in 'flow state'—where you find the work you're doing comes easy to you and time just washes by.

2 My 16-year-old daughter less so. Mercifully she stopped growing some time ago and her feet haven't grown since she was 12. Shoes are expensive.

Your metaphorical tool bag is brimming with years (decades?) of capability that's not getting used day to day, and sometimes, in a moment of calm reflection (or more likely in the car, on the train, or just as your head hits the pillow), you might have thought about what else you could do with it.

You may well be fed up. Fed up with corporate life, managers, brown nosing ('alignment'), and trying to get people to buy into your ideas who give less of a shit about you and your ideas than you can imagine. I'd describe that as corporate wankery.

Perhaps you've been made redundant. It happens, and it can be unpleasant. But it can also provide you with new options, maybe with a bit of extra money in your bank account.

Maybe you see self-employment as an opportunity to earn more, do more of what you enjoy, or balance home and work life your way. Or all three.

You may be bumbling along in a safe role and have just got fed up with it, but find yourself with no clear or obvious progression path even if you wanted one. And you wouldn't be alone: 80 per cent of people I asked about reasons for seeking a job change said their primary motive for leaving a business or role was not being stretched enough. Not because of pay, a boss who's a dick, or anything else.

Not being stretched enough.

I can confirm that going it alone at any stage of your career, no matter how you do it, is stretching.

What if you could channel that capacity for growth (personal, experience, income), and divert some of those skills, aptitudes, and knowledge from paid employment into building something of your own. Or at least taking a bit more control over your life.

Imagine having people or organisations (or both) pay you directly to help them better understand their problems and then solve them. Whether through a simple product like a two-page PDF tutorial or guide, through consulting sessions, or by working with them on an interim basis through your own limited company. Think about it.

If you've got this far through this introduction, the chances are you probably *have* thought about it. Perhaps quite a lot. But you need a shove in the right direction.

Why?
Because you're plagued with self-doubt.
You're scared of something.
You worry about failure. The financial risk.
And what people might think or say about you.
I mean, who would buy from you anyway?
And even if they did, what would you sell?

In short, you don't think you're enough.

But trust me (and all the other solopreneurs in all industries that have strapped in and gone for it): you are enough. And if you haven't received a lot of validating praise in your life, let me say it again.

YOU are enough.

You ARE enough.

You are ENOUGH.

YOU. ARE. ENOUGH.

This book is for you if you have desires on selling what you know, but don't feel you've got what it takes. But you want to go it alone. Enough is enough.

It's time for action.

YOU.
ARE.
ENOUGH.

WHO AM I, AND WHY AM I WRITING THIS (AND WHY SHOULD YOU TAKE ANY NOTICE)?

My name's Phil Sterne and I'm a coach. It feels weird to say it, but I help change people's lives. I want to help you get out of your own way, and if you don't know yet where you want to go—let alone what's in your way—I can help you find that too.

I wrote this book for two reasons.

1. **I want to be able to help more people change their lives.**
   The more people who buy this book (and the more that read it), the more people will receive the ideas and tools I'm going to describe and take some action to change their lives.

2. **I want to grow my own business.**
   This is part of my own journey from being an employee to becoming a service provider, and then an author. I want you to implement the contents of this book, but if you need support, you can come to me and we can talk about how I can help you.

I didn't always do this for a living. Working in recruitment, I'd never have described what I did as life changing for others, but on reflection, it may well have been. Helping them find the next role in their career, escape one they hated or weren't progressing in, or meet some other need in their life.

And I guess I've coached people over the years in one shape or another, but it was only in my second period of self-employment that doing it for a living became, well, a 'thing'.

My own journey to serving people in this way is what has caused me to reflect on the early days. Sticking with the journey metaphor, those early days felt like: "I think I want to go somewhere but I don't know where or how. I just know I don't want to be here."

Initially, at least, I wrote this book somewhat selfishly for *me*. But my past me. My 2014 me. The me that thought about going it alone but had all sorts of reasons (excuses) for not doing it. And then who did it anyway.

It's the book I could have done with to help give me the confidence and practical ideas to get going, and to lead me to the realisation that I wasn't alone.

By the time I set out on my own the first time, I'd bagged 17 years' experience of working for other people. It was hugely valuable. I learned how I enjoyed working, what I didn't enjoy working on, how I liked to be managed, how to manage myself, the environments I preferred, and so on.

One thing I knew was that I didn't like 'business as usual'. But I worked out that I enjoyed solving problems and making processes better, and getting people and businesses to think and act in a different way. My specialism was recruitment and all the activity that goes into it.

In 2014, I had a lot going on in my job and home life, and I was unknowingly about to break.

I don't think it's normal to get off a phone call and have to restrain yourself with all your might to stop yourself from throwing your mobile phone at the newly painted kitchen wall. I was LIVID. Someone at work had done the same thing again (and again) and, without realising it, I'd unwittingly built up so much stress that I had to release it. I went pop.

My boss and the company were great about it, and I took some time off. During that short period of convalescence I had a talk at the bottom of the garden with my wife. It was the furthest I'd travelled in some days.

"Why don't you go it alone?" she said, earnestly.

I scoffed at the idea.

We talked about me going into contracting (taking on short-term contracts and billing them a day rate for my time), but an outpouring of excuses followed. Reasons to not do that, rather than reasons to do it. Perhaps it was an immediate feeling of fear.

"I'm not good enough. And anyway, even if I was, I'm on three months' notice, and anyone hiring contractors needs you to start like next week."

And and and.

"What would I even do or sell? I don't know enough people to sell to even if I knew what I was selling. And why would anyone buy anything from me?"

"How are we going to afford to live? I can't just quit and cut off that salary. We need the stability." I was also the main breadwinner.

"Anyway I've got no idea what I'm doing, I don't know how to run a business." I was also experiencing a breakdown, so wasn't really able to think clearly.

And my mind spiralled out of control overthinking all the things I'd have to put in place to even begin thinking about working for myself.

Imagine a noisy pub with a band playing, fruit machines going off, and no soft furnishings. Or Piccadilly Circus at full tilt. That's what my head felt like.

Later in 2014, I resigned...and then almost immediately agreed to my first contract. With the same company, but three days a week. I'd project manage the implementation of a new recruitment system.

"This is what it's all about!" I thought to myself. "100 per cent of the income for 60 per cent of the time? Winner!"

I also landed another upcoming six-month contract to install a recruitment system, and they were happy for me to crack on at two days a week, remotely, to start getting up to speed.

I had no idea how to agree a contract though. More on that later.

Two years of day-rate contracting followed at a few different companies, each time stretching myself, meeting lots of new people, and learning (often the hard way) about the trials and tribulations of such work, before I tripped over a permanent job at Amazon in 2017. It seemed too good not to accept.

After a chunky role supporting the rollout of new warehouse buildings across Europe, in late 2019 I had another, more significant breakdown.

I took on a counsellor, had three months off, shed many, many tears, and was, by anyone's measure, empty. Completely numb. Induced by the stress of the role, the business, colleagues, and a less than flattering end of year review—I was broken.

By the start of 2020, pre-pandemic, I'd left Amazon. Nearly four months off had given me space to re-evaluate what I wanted to do with my life. At 45, I still had a lot to give. I was aware that at around the same age, Dad had a breakdown too. It cut his career short by at least 15 years. The strain on his mental health took such a toll that he never went back to work. And even earlier, at the age of 32, and having acquired many new skills in renovating our house, he'd considered switching careers from accountancy to becoming a builder. However, he was hit with M.E., and that idea went no further.

Something that came up as a green shoot during my counselling started to sprout further in my mind. What was I good at? What did I enjoy? What might people pay me for? What did people need?

I worked out that I loved helping people. All my career I had been helping them solve their problems, coaching them, supporting them, serving them. I enjoyed using my creativity, so could I use that in some way, whether in generating ideas, or physically through writing or artwork?

I'd had close to a 25-year career in recruitment. I could use that, rather than pivoting away altogether. What problems did people face? Well, for years I'd helped friends with their CVs, working out how to present their skills and experience for the jobs they wanted.

Then, BOOM!

I was starting up on my own again as a careers coach. And I haven't looked back.

Except to realise that the most testing periods are usually opportunities for us to grow. Or to find a new path. To have a refreshed purpose. Think of moorland wildfires decimating the plant life, the ash providing a rich soil and the clearing giving access to sunlight—allowing new green shoots to grow.

It had been horrific, that's for sure. But had it not happened, I wouldn't be doing what I am doing now. Like sitting in a pub on a Friday afternoon after my singing lesson, writing this book. Or holding a coaching session with a client while sat outside a countryside café. Or dipping in and out of my work to do something else. Because I can.

That's just my story. Yours will be completely different. You don't need to have had a breakdown or some catastrophic life-affirming event to finally re-evaluate your life, and decide working for yourself is the answer.

In fact, I absolutely hope you don't, and that you can take the steps ahead of time just because you want to, and can.

So what's your thinking behind considering going it alone, and more importantly why haven't you done anything about it yet?

It could be a combination of:

- low self-belief,
- the stories you've told yourself about who you are (and are not),
- you think you're too old (or too young),
- what you consider to be financial security,
- a lack of direction,

- limited appreciation of how to get going,
- the timing.

Now ask yourself, "What would I do if that wasn't an issue?".

What if instead you could have:

- robust self-belief,
- positive validation about your skills and the value you bring,
- a realisation that you can start something at any time of life,
- the understanding that you don't need loads of savings to start,
- direction on where you could take your business,
- guidance and multiple options on how to get going?

Don't you owe it to yourself to find a way? I mean, what's gonna be the result of doing nothing, and how will you feel in five years when you've still not done anything because you were too scared?

Well, we're going to spend the rest of the book dispelling some of those limitations, and opening your eyes to the real prospect of building an income that could potentially enable you to quit the rat race.

Do I have millions in the bank, a couple of Lamborghinis, and a place in Monaco?
No.

But do I have enough to consider myself successful, have more control over my time, and know that every bit of work I do is helping another human? Can I still go on skiing holidays, have fancy meals out, and within reason buy pretty much whatever I want (except a Ferrari)?
Yes.

Am I free of the shackles of corporate wankery?
Yes.

Do I have freedom to work where and when I want?
Kids and dog permitting, yes.

Am I worried about where next month's income is coming from?
Sometimes, but not especially. Still, a bit of fear stops me from being too complacent.[3]

But the work is ongoing. This isn't one of those "here I am writing this from a beach making £100K a month in my sleep" books. It's a slog, but a very worthy slog and one that I'll find ways of improving and making easier over time.

It is, however, the best version of my life that I could have imagined at the end of 2019. Had I dared to dream bigger sooner, if I'd have had the knowledge and skills I've developed in the last couple of years, and I'd have most likely taken the steps in this book earlier. But I didn't, and I'm more than cool with that because I've made them now, and I'm here to tell you about life on the other side.

So ask yourself: if we bumped into each other in three years and you told me you were living the most awesomest amazing life, what would you be telling me?

If any part of your answer would be working for yourself, or earning an income either alongside or without traditional 9-5 employment, then carry on reading.

Think about this for a second: most people spend decades making a living, rather than making a life.

Most people spend decades making a living, rather than making a life.

Don't they?

So, I'm going to take you through the 'reasons' (excuses) you might be giving yourself for not taking even the smallest of steps towards going out on your own.

I'll give examples and tell stories and of how you might approach resolving or disproving the limitations you are telling yourself that you have.

---

3 Of course, no one wants a slow month. But I have had many, and so will you, and it will well and truly kick your worry door in. But keep at it. See it as a data point to compare with next month, next quarter, next year. Each one you have and bounce back from will give you more evidence that you're going in the right direction.

And I'll show you real, actionable ways to get out there and will dare you to make a mark on the world, selling what you know to others who want to know it.

Ready?

LET'S GO!

MOST PEOPLE SPEND DECADES MAKING A LIVING, RATHER THAN MAKING A LIFE.

PART 1

WHAT'S STOPPING YOU FROM STARTING?

I GET IT.

You want to start out on your own, you really do. But you've so many niggles that are stopping you. The doubts. The damaging self-talk. The stories you tell yourself about who you are or what you are not.

Too many people go through life without getting anywhere near to reaching their potential (or knowing how much potential they have) because of the negative behaviours they learned, a lack of encouragement, or soul-crushing moments of criticism.

So they grow up feeling like they're not enough—and that fuels a lack of vision (and the courage to make that vision a reality).

Their relationship with money is often poor. Financial skills aren't taught in schools. Our young people don't learn the basics about budgeting and saving, let alone investing and compounding. Is it any wonder people worry about taking bold career steps that involve some financial risks?

As a population we're frequently encouraged to 'think big'—yet we're infrequently shown how to bridge the vast chasm between where we are now and the success on the other side. So we don't bother trying, as the task feels too big and the dream is killed before it's even taken shape into a set of ideas.

Part 1 will help you see where you might be holding yourself back, and give you the impetus and tools to back yourself and put some of those stories to bed. For good.

CHAPTER 1

THE STORIES YOU'RE TELLING YOURSELF.

In this chapter I'll take you through some of the stories that get in our way when considering working for ourselves.

The biggest story we tell ourselves, even if we don't use the specific words, is "I'm not good enough".

All those times you were picked on at school, or told by a teacher you weren't good enough to get a higher grade (and then did), or when some well-meaning (or not?) relative told you weren't much of an artist when you presented your drawing to them, or when you didn't feel you fitted in because you weren't into football, or when you made the best of it when you were managing the special sound effects at a school production and you shouted "crash bang wallop!" down the microphone because you couldn't find the tape with the actual crash sound effects on, or how you were made fun of because you had funny teeth when everyone else's were normal, or because you didn't wear the right trainers. True stories. It's just how it was.

Perhaps you didn't experience those things. Perhaps you did, or something else. But I did.

Now, this is absolutely not a sob story. I was very fortunate to grow up in a reasonably well-off, professional family. My parents grew up in working class communities, where they had to really graft for everything they had. They worked hard to make sure we didn't go without. They loved and cared for me and whilst we lived a fairly frugal life, money didn't seem to be a problem.

I did pretty well at school, but it was through bloody hard work that I achieved the results I did. I learned from this that not only do you get out what you put in but also (in my case at least) that parental support, guidance, and encouragement all play an important part.

I suppose what I'm saying here is that whilst I didn't live a bad life growing up, everything is relative. All these different levers—our parents' upbringing and own insecurities and strengths, how we're treated at school, the friends we make, our historic finances and relationships with money, and whether we live in a stable home with positive role models—they make us who we are.

We either build positive stories about ourselves, or potentially harmful, restrictive ones that that—whether we like it or not—become limiting beliefs. As we grow up, we gain our own experiences and we may see and hear things through our own eyes and ears that challenge, inform, or develop those values and stories. We'll either rebel against them or let them shape us. And sometimes they have to be unpicked by therapy. Sometimes they'll give us a magical internal power that we don't know we have until it's unlocked.

For me, having had a couple of instances where I quit my job with nothing to go to, and everything ultimately being OK, helped me forge a mindset that I could make leaps of faith and I'd be generally alright.

Our experiences create the stories we tell ourselves. What we're good at. What we're not good at. What we should do as a career, or not. What we should steer clear of doing because we have a history of fucking it up. How we thought we'd done something well but not everyone agreed. Or when we leant into a challenge, and it didn't go as planned.

We're simple creatures. Fight or flight. We're built to avoid danger. But I'm here to say, whatever your upbringing and that of the people who brought you up, and the life you've experienced to date, the opportunity is still there for the taking—the only thing getting in your way is YOU, your mindset, and some skills.

That's right. If you've been telling yourself that you're not the sort of person who could build and sustain a business income, you don't have to look very far to point the finger at the problem.

The more you tell yourself these things, the more they will become a self-fulfilling prophecy. The old adage of "whether you think you can or you think you can't, you're right" comes to mind here.

So let's start by exploring your mindset and investigating why you want to go it alone in the first place—this will help you start to build the vision of your potential future and create a foundation upon which to build your self-belief.

TASK 1—WHY?

Grab your notebook and separate a page into two columns. Or if it's a small book, just use two facing pages. Write: "Why I'd like to work for myself" on the top of the left column. Then jot down, in no particular order, why. Don't over-think it—there are no right or wrong answers here.

The second column is about making column one count. Build on what you've written. Say you've written "More money", write how much more, and by when.

Add why you've said that. What will that number do for you? Be specific.

Or if you've written "More flexibility over my time", say what you'd do with it. What it would free you up to do, and why that would be a good thing. Just go for it, and make it vivid, and make sure you write down why.

STRETCH TASK:

Take the why and ask why again. And again. When you get there, you'll have worked out the real reasons why it's important to you to take this step.

What are your reflections? Did you surprise yourself? How powerful do you feel as a result?

SUMMARY AND ACTION POINTS:

- Your story is your story. Acknowledge it, but it's in the past.
- Your future hasn't been written yet.
- Avoid using your past as a crutch for not taking action now.
- Listen to your stories. Then decide what you want to believe and what your next chapter will look like.

YOUR STORY IS YOUR STORY. ACKNOWLEDGE IT, BUT IT'S IN THE PAST.

CHAPTER 2
YOU HAVE LOW SELF-BELIEF.

"I can't do it. I'm not good enough.

What business would I have doing that? Stay in your lane, Phil!"

They're just a couple of the things I've told myself before. And you will have said similar things to yourself too.

Depending on the source you pick, the estimates (or research) will tell you that 75 per cent of the population suffer from imposter syndrome at some point in their life. Or that 58 per cent of people say they've experienced it. Or 66 per cent of people over 18 say they think they've had it.

The point is, imposter syndrome is as common as a sandwich at a tea party. My guess is that everyone doubts themselves at some point in their life.

I have. You have. Your boss has. Your parents have. Your kids have. Members of the royal family have. Billionaires have. Politicians have. People in every boardroom around the world have.

Some people cower to it, becoming so frightened of how it makes them feel that the only option is to do nothing. Others? After processing it, their only option is to lean into it and do it anyway.

The only thing that separates those two groups, then, is action.

Just how good does a person have to be to do something new?

People do this all the time, don't they. How? They probably do what I did and Google it. Or ask someone who knows more than them about it for some direction.

For example, I knew absolutely nothing about servicing my lawnmower. The bloody thing was putt-putting all over the place, hunting around for revs, not getting enough power or consistency to cut the grass.

I had three options:

1. **Find someone I could pay to sort it out.**
2. **Sort it out myself.**
3. **Buy a new mower.**

Now, my neighbour mentioned to me that his mower had been doing the same. He suggested some fuel additive and to change the oil, plugs, air filter, clean out the carb...and I'm like, "Er, did you confuse me for someone who knows their way around anything mechanical?"

Anyway, I had a word with myself. It went something like this:

"Phil. You're a big boy. It's a lawnmower, not a satellite. How hard can it be? There must be guides online. Someone will have posted a YouTube video of them doing it. Come on."

So, I searched for and watched some videos. Turns out there are many. I then searched for and bought a service kit, finding many to choose from.

Then I proceeded to badly follow the instructions in one of the YouTube videos. It took me plenty more time than I'd predicted (doesn't everything?), but I did it. I DID IT.

I serviced my mower, and now it works.

HOLDING YOURSELF BACK

I'd spent 30 years telling myself and anyone else I cared to tell that "I'm not mechanically minded", and then realised that a) I'd never tried and b) I'd never been trained. Nor had I sought out any form of relevant learning. Yet here I was, with bits of mower spread out over my lawn. And then I managed to put it back together again in the right places.

What did I really do? I felt the fear of fucking it all up and having to buy a new mower (my back up option 3)—and did it anyway.

Yes, it was harder than I thought. But would I do it again? Of course. What was missing before, then? Knowledge. I knew how to turn a screwdriver and a wrench. I just needed to know where to turn them and in what order.

And what of the people creating the lawnmower repair YouTube videos? They put them out there to serve people like me. For free. Because they could and they wanted to. They might have used them to build custom for their own repair businesses, as a lot of people will watch a video and still go...nah...and take it some place for repair anyway.

Rather than thinking "I'm not good enough" or "I don't know enough"—consider this: how many other people know as much about the thing you know about as you do? Fewer than you think. And how many have the guts to go out on their own? Fewer still.

The trouble is, our propensity to try something new is shaped by our life to date. If you've lived a life around people who have taken risks of any size and doing so has generally paid off (and when they haven't, they've bounced back and tried again a different way), you may be a bit less risk averse than someone who hasn't.

If you grew up in an environment where everything was kept very safe, and you were warned against dangers all the time, and there was no one around you challenging the status quo or doing anything differently, and instead they were worrying constantly about what other people think, I guess it could be in your make-up to be risk averse.

But then the opposite maybe true. You might have harnessed the behaviour you witnessed as a kid as fuel to strive to be different, and become the complete opposite of the people who cared for you, either out of an act of rebellion or a desire to carve your own path. And that could be the path of conformity, or the other path. The one where it's more difficult to see what's going to happen next. The riskier one.

Our ancestors might have considered 'a job for life' to be the ultimate in security. Come out of school, get a trade, and you'll have a job for life. Or go to school, gain a qualification and join a firm and you'll have a job for life.

When I started my recruitment career, I was astonished at the frequency with which I'd find myself talking to someone who'd been in the same company for 30 years. Or 40. Or more.

But these days, though those people do exist, changing jobs, changing employers, and even changing careers entirely is absolutely the norm. More people than ever feel empowered to do what's right for them.

TASK 2—WHY NOT?

Put yourself in a quiet space and give yourself 30 minutes. Leave your phone in another room.

In your notebook, draw two lines down the page ready to write three lists. The first list should be headed "Why I can't go and work for myself". This is a list of all the reasons you're telling yourself that you couldn't go it alone. Just get them out. In the second column, write why these reasons are valid. What makes you believe them so much?

Then with another pen in a different colour, imagine you are yourself in five years' time, looking back at those reasons having been successful in going it alone. In the third column, write down what you'd be saying to your five-years-younger self about those reasons.

Do they really make sense? What is the older (and wiser) you telling present day you? Are these fears real? Where did they come from? What does the older you now know that you don't today?

STRETCH TASK:

Add a further column—or just take another pen—and think about what your five-years-older self would be telling you if you *hadn't* taken steps to break free of corporate life. What are they saying?

SUMMARY AND ACTION POINTS:

- Everyone doubts themselves at some point in their life.
- Feeling imposter syndrome means you're doing something you're unfamiliar with, and you might get found out. Lean into it. It means you're growing.
- Everything you can do well today was a stretch for you at some point in your life. So stand further down the road of your life and look back at today—what would you tell yourself?
- Think about even the smallest risk you've taken. What was the outcome? What did you learn as a result?
- What would have been the outcome if you hadn't taken that risk?

CHAPTER 3

YOU DON'T REALISE HOW GOOD YOU ARE.

How many people want to be able to do the things you know how to do?
Lots, probably.

Would people pay you to know those things or learn those skills?
Of course.

You keep honing and honing and honing those skills or learning new ones. In the meantime, you're not sharing what you know with the people who are a few steps behind you.

How about this: what if I said you were effectively stealing from them by not sharing your knowledge?

And what if it wasn't about *you*? What if the many people out there that need your knowledge, experience, and guidance need it now?

Imagine that you have served someone powerfully with your expertise and knowledge, and that's enabled them to make a great step forward in their own journey. Do you have to know everything about that subject?
No.

No one knows everything about a subject. Some know more than others, and it's the former that teaches the latter.

Your potential customers might only need to know the first few steps to get going. Usually there's one thing that gets in people's way of doing something.

And that is not starting. So what if you can put in front of them the basics for them to simply get started?

Think about that for a second.

They know nearly nothing about their chosen subject. Like, say, servicing a lawnmower (bear with me).

You, on the other hand, may not service lawnmowers for a living, but you'd love to, and you do know how to do it. So you put out a YouTube video for people who don't.

Then you put out another video on how to remove and sharpen the blade.

And another on how to mow a lawn properly.

And. And. And.

You develop a following. People start asking you for more videos. You make them, they give you great feedback. You then start offering to service and repair people's mowers for them.

MAKING IT UP

In three years, what's your dream? To run a lawnmower servicing business employing a team of people servicing and prolonging the life of mowers? Salvaging and fixing otherwise perfectly good mowers and selling them? I don't know, I'm just making shit up.

But guess what?

That's what everyone else in business is doing. Particularly the freelancers and people running businesses of all sizes. They know some stuff and they make up what people might want to buy. They look for gaps in people's knowledge and skills, and the problems they have, and work out if they can charge for it.

They put some things out there, simple offers, things that don't take a lot of time to create. They might just share free knowledge on social media to gauge interest and build credibility, authority, and an audience first.

Amazon are at the other end of the scale here, and they sell products—but think of the Echo Dot. They innovated that because they thought their customers would buy it. And they did. There have been plenty of other innovations they've created behind the scenes that only made it to test audiences, and some that didn't even make it that far.

They're making shit up, every day. And you can too.

So...ask yourself, what do you know that other people don't know, but want to know? Then find a way to package it and sell it.

When I started my second solopreneurial[4] journey, I didn't really think it would turn into something that would comfortably pay not only for our general living expenses, but to enable things like holidays and meals out.

Maybe those low expectations helped me.

I started small. I was just doing something that ticked my 'why' boxes, and it went from there.

I had 25 years' experience of recruiting. Reading and selecting CVs. Building recruitment teams, systems, and processes. I knew a thing or two—and tons more than your average job seeker.

Guess what a job seeker wants more than anything? A job. And how do they get that? Through having a CV that gets them an interview. How do they get one of those? Either write it themselves or follow the guidance of someone who's been doing it for years. Will they pay for it? Some won't, but...some will.

How do you build enough trust with those people to assure them you'll do a good job?

4 Apologies if the word "solopreneur" makes your teeth itch.

Start small. Write LinkedIn posts that help people solve their problems. Put out YouTube videos. Get testimonials from early customers you've helped at a low cost or even for free—then screen grab and share the crap out of them.

Keep giving value. And more value. And tell people they can work with you. Give them permission to contact you. Share tales of people who have been successful after working with you, or using the knowledge in your videos, templates, or guides.

TASK 3—WHAT?

Write another list. Or draw a picture or brainstorm it—whatever works for you.

If a random stranger (like me) asked you to tell them the headlines of the things you're good at, what would you tell them? Write it all down.

These could be broken into technical skills, people skills, soft skills. What can you do that other people around you find difficult?

Are you the person that other people come to sort out their spreadsheets? Are you a slide deck genius? Are you the ideas person? Do you ask the most insightful questions? Are you a report writer? Can you shine a light on the problem no one else has seen? Are you quieter and more diligent than everyone else?

What do people ask you for help with? In your group of friends and colleagues, which 'one' are you?

What is your 'weird'? The thing that makes you a bit different? Do you look at the world in a different way to other people? Do you think of the things others don't?

Write it all down.

These are the things you can do that other people might want to pay you to show them how to do.

STRETCH TASK:

If your current boss asked you to come up with an idiot-proof guide in a one-pager tomorrow for some aspect of your job, to teach someone in a different team how to do it, what would it be?

Could you turn that into a PDF that someone else in the world would find useful? I'll bet you could.

SUMMARY AND ACTION POINTS:

- No-one knows everything about a subject. Some know more than others, and it's the former that teaches the latter.
- You're better than most of the population at what you know about.
- You're certainly better than the people who need your services.
- People will pay to learn things from people that are a few steps ahead of them on a similar journey.
- Everyone is making it up on the daily. It's OK.
- Work out what you know that other people don't know, but want to know. Find a way to package it and sell it.
- Ask not "Am I good enough?" but "What practical skill do I need to learn to put what I already know into the world?"

CHAPTER 4

YOU'RE WORRIED ABOUT WHAT OTHER PEOPLE WILL THINK.

We're creatures of ego, and creatures of self-preservation.

In all of pre-history, if our ancestors showed up differently to others, they might have been seen as a threat. And the only good threat to be, was the threat to the food that was walking about.

If you were different for some other reason, then you'd probably die early. If you weren't fast enough, savvy enough, accurate enough, attractive enough, strong enough, or caring enough—well you'd either be killed by the very animal you're trying to kill for food, or be killed by another animal that saw you as food. Or have a reduced likelihood of eating the best food, occupying the best living quarters, or mating. At all. And that would mean your line would die out.

This plays out all over humanity today.

Turning up at a social event wearing something other than the social uniform. Having an opinion that's different to everyone else. Standing out because you have a different skin colour to everyone around you, or have a disability, or for being a woman in a stereotypically male industry.

If you're different, you can feel exposed. And no-one particularly wants to die or not mate because of it. So all too often we conform for the sake of the status quo, masking what we really feel about how we show up in the world.

I spoke to a guy this morning who is considering setting up a used car sales business.

He's come from a corporate background, and left his very well-paid leadership role when the company changed hands. So what's next for him?

To quote him quoting me, he said "Phil, zero part of me is looking forward to stepping into another company. I just find the corporate wankery exhausting."

Now, I know this book is primarily aimed at those of you who want to set yourself up as a knowledge worker, but you might be wrestling the same ego and self-preservation questions as Mike (not his real name) was.

When we dug around in the risks involved in following through on his plan, other than the financial risk, he cited potential reputational damage if it didn't work out, and what his friends, family, and ex-colleagues would think of him stepping out as a used car dealer "and the stigma that brings".

Well here are the five reflections I shared with him:

1. **Who gives a fuck what anyone else thinks?** If you're doing this for YOU, and your family, then what someone else may or may not think about your chosen path is of no concern of yours.

2. **The only opinions you need to care about are those of your potential customers.** Just make sure you offer them the best service available in the niche you operate in and drive positive word-of-mouth.

3. **Truth bomb—you're not that important.** People have got enough going on inside their own heads thinking about themselves to be thinking too hard about you. Sorry. So they might not be thinking anything.

4. **If they do take a moment to think about your life choices, they might just be in admiration of your balls.** It takes gumption and conviction to go out and do something different, to step away from what's often considered as the 'normal' path of working for someone else. But all you're doing when you're working for someone else is helping *them*

achieve *their* dream, and at some point in the dim and distant past, *they* stepped out and decided to create something new for themselves too.

5. **As well as admiration, they might just be envious.** Envious because really, they'd love to become their own boss, take their dream to market, or just come out of the corporate world and do something different—because life is there for the taking. They might be envious because they believe (perhaps wrongly) that they could never take that kind of 'risk'—whatever their risk is.

As easy as it is for me to sit here and tell you why you shouldn't pay too much attention to what other people have to say, you do need to be prepared for what people might say when you tell them what you're doing. But be careful who you listen to.

Paul Rayner was my first boss when I started my recruitment career. He talked to me about the difference between 'give up' goals and 'go up' goals. An example of a 'give up' goal might be to give up something that's bad for you—like smoking, drinking, or negative self-talk.

Telling people around you might just help you achieve that goal. Getting in the mindset of being a non-smoker is important for the next time you get offered a cigarette.

"No thanks, I don't smoke."

Done, clear as a bell. And hopefully people around you will support you. They might ask you why, but that's none of their business. Your choice to make that change. But in the main it's the sort of goal other people can get behind.

A 'go up' goal, however, is aspirational. In the smoking example it might be "I want to be healthy and live a long life so I can see my grandchildren grow up". And the thing with aspirations is that they are different for everyone. Some might aspire to be a world-famous mountaineer. Others, to run a multimillion-pound business. Why they want to do that thing is their call.

For others, the height of their aspirations might be to simply have a safe place to sleep at night. It's all relative.

But the people around you—the ones happy going to work for someone else everyday—well they won't necessarily share your aspirations to be free of the corporate world and do something for yourself, whatever your motivations.

And because of that, and their own belief systems around personal limitations and risk, they might be surprised to hear what you have to say. They might say "What do you want to go and do that for? You were earning a fortune/well respected/and, and. Are you sure?"

They might (however well-meaning) try to sow more seeds of doubt in your mind[5], and you might start questioning your own decision making, or try to justify your thinking. It's also entirely possible that they are huge risk takers too, more so than you, and will blindly cheer you on without consequence.

Neither of these groups contain people you want to openly share your plans with if you're expecting useful guidance or feedback.

"But I'm going mad in my head, Phil!"

Sure you are. Well as part of your own due diligence and scoping out what you want to do, find someone, or two or three people in your network that you could call trusted, unbiased advisors. A critical friend. Perhaps they've done something similar before, or know your market better than you, or may give you pause for thought about your numbers.

They are the voices you need to be listening too, not the ones in your head that are holding you back, or those of certain friends and family who don't know the first thing about your business. However, some friends or family *might* know the first thing about your business. I'd urge you to consider engaging them only if you're certain they can be objective.

---

5 Seeds of doubt are OK—but only if they're useful and open up a line of enquiry you can investigate objectively.

You could also seek out a coach to help you explore what's going on in your head and make sense of it, consider scenarios, and think about angles you've not yet thought about.

Final point. Do you think that some of Jeff Bezos' friends, family, and ex-colleagues thought he was nuts starting up an online bookstore from his garage? ***Probably.***

SUMMARY AND ACTION POINTS:

- Be careful about the voices you choose to listen to—both of others and your own.
- Expect people to have different reactions to your ideas and plans—but remember they're not always going to share your passion or enthusiasm. They'll be passionate and enthusiastic about something else that's important to them.
- Find experts to become your trusted advisors or critical friends.

CHAPTER 5

YOU DON'T THINK YOU'RE BRAVE ENOUGH.

So what are you telling yourself about bravery?

A friend of mine once said to me: "Fair play Phil, I don't know how you do it. You've got balls. I've got a mortgage and three kids, and a decent salary that I'd have to give up to go out on my own."

This is a confident guy. Great at what he does, and so much more. Super likeable. Knows his shit on a range of subjects to a level of borderline geekery that he acknowledges and loves.

Yet I hadn't really considered that the steps I'd taken had required balls. Well, maybe a bit, but I guess everyone's value systems, comfort zones, and boundaries are different. That's what makes humans amazing creatures. We all look at things through different lenses.

So, when I talk of bravery, I realise that everyone is coming from a different starting point.

As a young man, I was incredibly fearful of rejection. There'd be the lads who had no problems chatting up girls and getting laid, then there was me. I'd never really had the positive reinforcement that such an endeavour would yield results. I asked girls out, for sure, just not very often.

Yet with the value of hindsight and age, a young man out to get laid simply has to play the numbers. It ceases to be about bravery or fear of rejection.

Phrases like "the more girls I ask out, the luckier I get" and "always talk to the hottest girl in the room" resonate here because to me even thinking about doing this would have been way out of my comfort zone. But consider the hottest girl in the room: she either is pig sick of dickheads chatting her up, or she just gets almost no attention (other than drooling eyes) because most guys would consider her to be out of their reach.

But, you won't know unless you try.

"What if she says no? I just don't think I could take that kind of rejection," were the words that came out of George McFly's mouth in *Back To The Future,* when Marty was trying to get him to ask his mum, Lorraine, to go to 1955's Enchantment Under The Sea Dance. He said the same thing 30 years later when Lorraine suggested he send his amazing book idea to a publisher.

But that moment in fight or flight, when his well-practised set piece punch came to pass (by having to lay out his nemesis, Biff, for real) he stepped up to the plate. He clenched his fist and swung a punch that floored Biff, amazed everyone around him, and he got the girl. He'd stood up not only for himself, but his values. And his attitude and belief system changed from that day on. He'd taken a risk, wildly outside his comfort zone, and it paid off.

Cut back to 1985, and there's Biff cleaning George's car. George is married to Lorraine. He's become a successful writer. His kids have been raised in a positive environment with great role models and developed solid careers of their own.

What might be your 'punch Biff in the face and change your life' moment? Has it happened yet? If not, what step could you take that represents a shift in your bravery?

If you're not quite ready for that, what smaller step could you take that requires a bit less bravery? And what actions can you take to make that step less risky?

Often the answer can be found in skills and knowledge. Because those two combined can be a powerful force. Complement them with a track record of success, perhaps from taking small steps that have built up your resilience or eased your mind, and things you previously thought would require bravery seem less risky or difficult.

When I had a mini breakdown in 2014, I narrowly stopped myself from launching my phone into my kitchen wall.

When I had that walk down the garden with my wife and she said, "Why don't you just go out on your own?", my immediate instinct, in a brain-addled moment of frustration, anger, and feeling absolutely fucking useless at my job, was: "I don't know nearly enough to go out on my own". I felt the fear. I wasn't feeling brave.

And that was in part because I had no idea how this world worked. *What would I even do?* Did she mean set up a business as an independent recruitment consultant? Or find a way of working for a company solving recruitment-flavoured problems without being an employee? I used the feeling that I didn't know enough about anything as an excuse. I didn't know anything about:

- the required skills of a business owner,
- what they got paid (or how),
- setting up a limited company (or if it was necessary),
- business banking,
- VAT and tax (personal or business),
- websites,
- logo design,
- etc. etc. etc.

But instead of throwing a stack of paper in the air, becoming completely overwhelmed, and shouting "it's fuck-this-shit o'clock" (although I was close to this, especially given my state of mind), I started doing some research. I turned all those barriers into questions I needed to learn the answers to.

- What sort of opportunities are out there?
- How do people 'work'?
- How much do clients pay?

- Do I need a limited company?
- Do I need a business bank account?
- Do I need to be registered for VAT?
- Do I need a website?
- How do I arrange all the above?

That was just the tip of the iceberg.

I needed to put my big boy pants on and build courage. With all these questions, I was running before I could crawl, let alone walk.

What if telling myself "I can't do that because I don't know enough about..." was a sign that I just had to go and learn something?

It felt like a leap, but I started by doing some research. My initial thought was to become a virtual recruitment manager for small-to-medium sized businesses. The common, modern way of describing working this way is 'fractional'. Fractional in so far as I'd not be full time anywhere, but supporting multiple businesses as their Fractional Recruitment Business Partner/Head of Resourcing/Talent Acquisition Director etc. Perhaps a day a week, maybe eight days a month. But I'd work for them for a fraction of the time.

I thought I'd help them get their careers websites and selection processes working properly, manage their recruitment needs, and improve how they did recruitment in all sorts of different ways.

I found that firms were recruiting interim contractors to run recruitment process improvement projects for them. But—and this was the big but—they wanted people to start next week.

I spoke to the recruiters to check. And yes, they absolutely did want someone to start in the next couple of weeks. But damn, I was on three months' notice! How could I possibly make that work?

All was not lost. I used those conversations to suss out answers to my other questions and build my knowledge (and courage!). Questions like:

What sort of contracts are out there?
Recruitment systems implementation projects, branding work, maternity cover contracts—all sorts.

Do I need a limited company and business bank account to make job applications?
No, not always—often the agency would subcontract you through what they call an umbrella company.

Do I need a website?
No.

Do I have the skills?
Absolutely!

The rest I could sort out later.

Despite the issues with notice periods and my availability, all the research and conversations pointed towards me becoming an interim contractor. A recruitment manager or project manager gun-for-hire. Charging day rates. Big ones. That was the only way I could see it working. Delivering change projects, hiring assignments, whatever—for companies not big enough to have a dedicated recruiter or larger firms simply needing temporary professional resource.

There were huge risks. My salary and the mortgage were the two biggest concerns. Contracts getting cut short. Gaps between them. Not even landing one in the first place!

Fortune favours the brave, I thought. I am bloody good enough. And I found out the answer to the "How much do they pay?" question was that day rates were often double what I was earning as a salary. Double!

If I failed, I could just get another permanent job. I had some savings. I could sell the car and get a cheaper one. We could even downsize the house. There were all sorts of options—but in any event I would be happier than I was in that job at that time.

I had confidence in the number of interim contracting jobs out there and agreed with my wife that even if it meant travelling or being away for days at a time, we'd make it work. But I'd need to resign with nothing to go to and get them to shorten my notice period so I could get myself in the running for these opportunities ASAP.

The day came. I resigned. I told them I was going out on my own. I backed myself, and with just a few months' savings, I went for it.

My boss immediately asked me to stay on as a contractor to implement the project that had coincidentally just been given the green light. Unbelievable.

They couldn't afford (or hadn't budgeted) to pay any more for me than my actual salary with all the national insurance costs and whatnot. So I broke that number down and we settled on me working three days a week, on the same pay. But this time I was invoicing monthly.

Here are some of the further questions I found the answers for—all the time building my courage and self-belief:

1. **How do we contract?**
   The company already had a standard Contract for Services to use and agree on. To do that, I could either represent myself as a sole trader, or effectively offer my services via my own limited company. That sounded daunting and a bit 'grown up'. But come on, I was 39 years old for fuck's sake. Remember those big boy pants?

   I'd been recommended an accountant to talk to about setting up a company. We discussed the pros and cons of being a sole trader versus forming a limited company and the tax benefits of each. I spent hours on contractor forums, asking questions, picking up titbits of knowledge from those who'd been contracting for years. It was enough information. You might need more, or less, but you'll work out which approach is best for you.

   I went limited because I took the view that it looked more professional to charge myself out through the business as a consultant, and of course

I was covered by the limited liability of the company. Also, I knew I'd be able to put many costs of operating my business against my profits and reduce the business's tax burden. You can do that as a sole trader too, but I preferred the idea of keeping everything separate.

2. **Do I need a business bank account?**
   Well for me, going down the limited route, I wanted to separate my personal finances from those of the business. So, yes, I did need a business bank account. I researched again and set up one with my existing High Street bank because I thought it would be easier. The second time around setting up a business, I used one of the new breed of app-based business banks which has been a hundred times easier and quicker to set up and administer day-to-day.

   If sole trading is your route, ask your accountant or bookkeeper for advice on how to bank.

3. **Do I need to be registered for VAT?**
   Not necessarily, unless you're going to be billing (turning over) more than the HMRC threshold—check the HMRC website for the current information (and to check if your services attract VAT in the first place, as not all do). At the time of writing, you can turn over £90,000 before you need to charge VAT on your invoices. If you don't live in the UK, please seek advice on your domestic business tax arrangements.

What happened next?

I'd already been applying for other contract jobs in the background. They were full-time positions. Incredibly, I interviewed for one (and only one), they liked me, saw the value I could add, and we contracted up on the basis I'd do two days a week (largely remotely) while I was still working through the other contract.

Winner! And I'm still in touch with my first real client and we remain friends.

I recognise that all of this might sound very easy. I can assure you it wasn't. It felt a like wading through a swimming pool of baked beans. I think at best I can say I was fortunate, but there were plenty of times that it felt like my gig applications were falling into a black hole.

If you've been trodden down by your current working experience, or something else in your life, you might feel completely destroyed and unable to face day-to-day basics, let alone work.

When you're coming from this kind of place, where perhaps the 'I've had enough' moment has sneaked up on you and not so much tapped you on the shoulder but bludgeoned you about the head with a scaffold pole, it can be difficult to make positive tracks.

The apparent sheer magnitude of the mountain in front of you can be overwhelming when, to drag out the metaphor, you're underwater in the lake next to the mountain.

So when thoughts like "I don't even have a company, a name, a website, a logo, a bank account, etc." cross your mind, they could easily be enough to make you overthink it all and procrastinate or even dismiss it, favouring the path well-trodden. If you're struggling with your mental health, they could become total blockers to making any positive steps forward at all.

Take my advice on this one—just simplify. You don't need all that stuff. You don't need to try and do everything at once. You just need to start by having conversations with people in your niche. Other service providers. Recruiters (if you're looking at getting hired as a contractor). Potential clients.

One of the earliest readers of this book, Rachel, was made redundant after 23 years in the same business. After reading this, she took herself off to a local networking event. She had no expectation of winning clients, and in fact she didn't even really know what she was going to say to people. She just wanted to go, soak it up, listen, and learn.

And before she knew it, Rachel was having a conversation with someone about how she was thinking of going it alone as a marketing consultant. The person she was talking to knew someone who had a need, and put them together.

They became her first client.

No business cards, websites, LinkedIn company profiles, bank accounts, limited companies—none of it. Just start with conversations.

There's more (much more) about becoming a contractor (as one of several approaches to going it alone) later in the book.

HOW CAN I BECOME 'MORE BRAVE'?

Often, when we think about taking a big leap of any kind, our brain sends out signals to protect us by reminding us of what we stand to lose. Security and status are usually high on the list.

So the common response (and one I had too when I started thinking about going it alone) was "Yeah, sounds great, but what if I fail?"

I discovered that I was *afraid*. And you too might be afraid.

Afraid of failure.
Afraid of not knowing what to do next.
Afraid of what other people would say or think.
Afraid of how you'd keep a roof over your head.
Afraid of how you'd pick yourself up if it went wrong.

Well, here's an insight for you. These scenarios are every bit as much in your own head as what you imagine to be the perfect life. The only way the nice picture can EVER happen is if you take some positive steps towards it. Isn't it?

It's not going to happen on its own. But what are the options? You stay doing the same shit you've been doing for years and get the same outcome, or take even the smallest of tentative steps into the outside world towards that goal?

I heard a podcast recently featuring organisational psychologist and author Adam Grant (it was one of Steven Bartlett's *Diary Of A CEO* series). He touched on the concept of 'cognitive entrenchment'.

Think "we've always done it this way". Cognitive entrenchment is what can happen when you become increasingly experienced at something, and you become stuck in your ways or entrenched in your thinking.

Apply that to your career for a second. You've lived it for so many years, moving from one job to another, and perhaps from company to company.

You get bored with a job, fed up with a boss, you feel underpaid, or it just no longer fits with your circumstances. Following "we've always done it that way" thinking, your next step is to tart up your CV, add your latest job to it, and fire it off in response to some adverts.

You know how to get out of your job and find another, as the path is well worn, isn't it? But then what happens? You get a new job and a few years down the line (or sooner), the same happens again. And your cognitive entrenchment tells you "This is the way".

Here's another thing. All the time you're doing this, you also think you're in control. You get to choose how you lay out your CV, what jobs you apply for, which offers you accept. Yeah?

How about this then: What if I said you're not in control because you're only applying for the jobs that are presented to you? You're just deciding what looks interesting (or not). I've lost count of the times I've heard people say "I applied for that job even though I didn't really want it".

The real choice comes from deciding what kind of work you want to do, with whom, and for how long. Then you are able to make real decisions, based on your own thinking and with *intention*, rather than on what's put in front of you.

However, it's scary. And not easy. And, in all truth you might not be suited to building a business of one person. But you certainly won't know if you can swim if you don't you dip your toe in the water first. Entrepreneurs also don't stop at one business, do they? They try umpteen different things and fail A LOT before hitting on the thing that's going to fly.

Emerging from that cognitive entrenchment might take some work. And the biggest thing you're likely to be thinking about is everything you stand to lose by going it alone—and then failing.

TASK 4—ARE YOU A LOSER?

Here are two questions:

1. **What do you have to lose?**
2. **What do you stand to gain?**

Let's work backwards. Ideally you want an hour to yourself. Longer if you want to make a really good stab at it. I did say you'd need to do some work.

If we bumped into each other in say, three years, and you said to me "Fucking hell Phil, my life has changed. It's amazing. You won't believe what I'm up to now! I've just had the most amazing 12 months!" ...what would you be telling me?

Start to paint the picture in your head. Write it down. Or draw it. But commit it to paper.

- Where are you living in the world?
- Who are you with?
- What are you doing day to day?
- What experiences have you had?
- What are you doing to earn money—and how much?
- What are you doing with your free time?
- How do you FEEL about all of this?
- What do your friends and family think about it (if you care)?

This is what you have TO GAIN.

On another page, write down all the things that drain you of energy now. And the things in your life that you want to get away from. Use the same prompts as above if you like, or come up with new ones. You have probably worked out where this is going.

Yep. That is what you stand TO LOSE.

Let's twist that around for a second and think about this another way.

Rich Litvin and Steve Chandler, in their book *The Prosperous Coach*, talk about goals being something you can *come from*, rather than working towards.

Yeah, I didn't get it either initially either. Let me explain through this stretch task:

STRETCH TASK:

Bring back the list or picture of an amazing three years into the future. Imagine we're still stood there talking, and I ask you:

"What actions are you taking that are different to back then?"

"What do you know now that you didn't know then?"

"What skills have you built that you didn't have then?"

You've just given yourself a blueprint for actions and models of behaviour that you can take TODAY.

While you are still employed. Or doing whatever you are doing. You don't have to wait three years. Focus on what you already have.

Here's an example.

Say I paint this simple yet glorious picture of three years' time:

I'm sat with my wife and family, in a small timber bungalow, with a roaring firepit, overlooking a beach. It's sunset and we're in Bali. The kids are at university now, but we paid for them to come over for a holiday with us to our bolthole.

We spend several weeks at a time out here, we can both still work remotely, and I'm billing £400K/year in coaching. I've served 200,000 people with personal coaching and all my tools, downloads, and social media content.

I can work when I want. My clients are in two camps—senior people looking to leave the rat race and set up on their own, and senior people progressing their careers into executive and non-executive director roles. I am serving them powerfully and most of my business comes from referrals. I have three books published that are selling well and feature in the main bookshops.

I'm making a small side income from playing guitar and singing in bars, though I mostly do that for fun rather than the money.

I feel like things have gone outrageously well, I've taken big steps to get here, and learned a lot. My friends wonder how the fuck I did it and think I live a life of Riley. Perhaps I do. I feel like all roads have led to this point. I feel rich in life as well as financially stable.

Sounds great eh? It does to me anyway. And yours will sound great to you too. Make it as rich as you can. When you think you've finished, ask yourself "What else?". Try to avoid too many material lists of 'I wants'. Look for how you're living life, the experiences you're having, and how you're serving your customers.

But here's a thing. I've never been to Southeast Asia, unless you can call a couple of days in Hong Kong on the way back from Australia in 2004 'going to Asia'. In fact, I just had to Google Bali to make sure I was in the right place. It's in Indonesia.

To make it anything like a reality, you have to use the dream as something to come from.

So asking those questions again, or others, will tell you what you need to do and who you need to be and what skills you need and...and.

Now you can build the answers to all these questions into your life today. Here's some of mine:

"What sort of person am I?"
Someone who generates an income from his experience and knowledge, who is doing things in his life that he enjoys. I serve people to help them live fantastic lives.

"Who are my clients?"
Senior people from around the world who are struggling with getting to where they want to get to in life, or don't quite know where that place is.

"How did I find them?"
By referral and inbound marketing, and consistently connecting with new people. Creating value-driven content on LinkedIn and YouTube, providing high-quality coaching experiences that have built a word-of-mouth business.

"What services am I providing?"
One-to-one and group coaching services, helping people live all facets of their lives better. I have authored three books, post near-daily LinkedIn content, and write a fortnightly blog, as well as uploading new videos to YouTube every month.

"Where am I living?"
In the UK, with a holiday home in Devon, and I'm looking at some places in Bali.

"What actions am I taking every day that are different to back then?"
Connecting with new people and building relationships from initially small interactions, in far greater numbers than I ever did back then. I am charging my clients £50,000 to coach them.

"What do I know that I didn't know then?"
That having a flashy website is not nearly as important as getting out and talking to people and giving them a valuable experience of what you can offer.

Where Bali is, how much property costs, and how to go about buying it. How Bali compares to other Southeast Asian locations for a part-time home.

How to confidently say some of the biggest numbers I've ever said to potential clients when telling them my fees.

"What skills have I built that I didn't have then?"
I can remember more song lyrics and chords through consistent practicing and have all but conquered stage fright through repeatedly appearing at open-mics and booking small solo gigs.

My coaching capability has gone from strength to strength through repeated practice. I know how to consistently create clients.

Do you see how I've just written the blueprint for the actions I can take next? This is an abridged version. There is plenty of scope here to go into much more detail, and I recommend you do. The more richly you paint it in your mind, the clearer it is for you to visualise and assess the gap between where you are now and where you want to get to.

We're often most afraid of the things we want most. Or afraid they won't match up to our ideals, or that we'll fail trying. Or...afraid that we just don't know where to start, so we get clogged up in a malaise of procrastination.

So look back at what you've written and highlight three things:

1. **things you're doing already,**
2. **things you could start doing very easily,**
3. **the 'stretch' goals.**

You may well find you're closer to being 80 per cent of your target self than you think.

And with those items in (1) above, what would happen if you did more of them?

The items in (2) above, what's the smallest step you can take to do just one of those things?

And with (3), think about why they're important to you. You can see from my own example I'd need to undertake some real research to confirm to myself that Bali is the destination of choice. Where else could I go to get a similar feeling? Why Bali? Why not somewhere else?

Doing this will help you assess the importance of the thing you think would be amazing. Do the research. Finally, critically assess what you've written. Turn it on its head.

Ask yourself, what will hinder this future becoming a reality? Going back to the start of this chapter, the voice that was saying "Yes Phil but what if I fail?"— if you're going to fail, these are likely culprits. Write them out and work out what's gonna get in your way:

- things you do,
- habits you have,
- the way you think,
- things people might say,
- external factors—like the market for your product.

This is harder. It is hard to critically assess yourself (and yes, I can help you through it), but it's a valuable exercise.

Having the self-awareness to think about what's going to get in your way, or might be enough (and it only needs to be just enough) to push you off your path, or dissuade you from taking the smallest action to get going—knowing and being able to see that for what it is will help you recognise it, acknowledge it, and keep on going.

SUMMARY AND ACTION POINTS:

- Define your 'punch Biff' moment.
- Break down big goals into small steps.
- Turn obstacles into learning opportunities.

- Visualise your life three years into the future.
- Identify energy drains.
- Build a blueprint for action.
- Continuously evaluate and adjust.

CHAPTER 6

YOU DON'T THINK IT'S THE RIGHT TIME.

Is it ever?

They say the best time to start was back then, second best is now. But is that really true?

You'll never know, because that time in the past has passed. If there was an opportunity back then, you didn't take it, so there's no point in ruminating over it. So logically, the next best time to make the step you want to take could be *now*.

There are probably a few other things getting in your way though.

They're causing a tension.

You don't feel ready. Maybe you think you're:

- too old,
- too young,
- too entrenched,
- expecting a bonus,
- not experienced enough yet,
- likely to get a promotion soon,
- going on a holiday in six weeks,
- gonna have your mortgage go up,

- too involved in some other project,
- possibly going have a new boss next month.

Yadda yadda yadda.

Let me say these words:

THERE. IS. NEVER. A. GOOD. TIME.

So there's never a better time than now.

You're too old? I hear people in their 20s saying this as much as those in their 50s. "Oh, I'm 27 now so that ship has sailed", or "Well, if I'd have done that when I was 19..."

You're too young? Really? So what stops the kid who makes and sells lemonade on the street outside their house, or sells their toys at a car boot sale, or who does the other kid's homework for them for money?

Guess what? If you have knowledge of how to do something, and that something is something someone else would like to know, it doesn't matter how old (or young) you are.

Stop using your age as a limitation. It's yours and yours only. No one else cares.

Sure, everywhere you look you see young entrepreneurs who have seized a moment in time, with a given set of skills, some balls-out confidence, and have gone for it. And turned it into Facebook, Airbnb, or something else.

Do you think they were ready enough? Really?

Of course they weren't. They were probably no more than 80 per cent ready. Perhaps only 60 per cent.

Let's look at the world of software development for a moment. Software is rarely released as a full bells-and-whistles product. Usually there'll be a holding product, known as a minimum viable product, or MVP, that meets the core customer requirements.

And that's it. Consider it a usable proof of concept.

If you continue to wait for 'the right time' and having the perfect set of skills to take to market, you'll never do it. Because you're focusing on the wrong thing.

If instead of thinking "What small bit of my skills and expertise would someone pay for?" you're thinking "I really need to have mastered everything in this niche or I won't be taken seriously" then you'll never do it.

Every niche evolves. Start small and just do something. Find your MVP. A one-page guide. A set of social media posts. A video you shot on your phone. A three-point LinkedIn post saying: "*The 3 problems* [your target customer] *faces when they* [their target outcome]." Then giving your readers three things they can do about it. I'll talk more about this later in the book.

This is about just starting, and avoiding over-complicating everything.

The fact you're even thinking about it and reading this book tells me you're ready. Right now. Not tomorrow, not next month, or next year.

NOW.

"Yeah, but Phil, this is a young person's game. I've got too much at stake now."

That bullshit button is getting a workout today, isn't it?

Just this week I saw a post on LinkedIn about a guy called Kev who switched careers...at 70.

Yep.

50 years prior he'd been a mineshaft engineer (pretty niche), switched careers to sales, and his success in that gave him the shove to set up and run his own cleaning business.

But then at 70, he decided he wanted something different. So he put his lifelong interest in physical health to work and trained to become a personal trainer. Yes, you read that correctly. You've just re-read it to make sure, haven't you?

Here's another. You've probably read the Colonel Sanders story. He'd been a steam engine stoker, a railway labourer, and then a filling station operator when he moved to Kentucky. During the great depression, Shell offered him a filling station to run rent-free in return for a percentage of sales.

Early in the 1930s, he started serving fried chicken dishes out of his living quarters adjacent to the filling station, before opening a restaurant.

He worked out and patented a way of pressure frying the chicken, but he didn't think of franchising the business until much later, and in 1952 the first franchise opened in Utah. He was 62 years old. When the rapid growth became overwhelming for him, the Colonel sold the business—at age 73.

You really can take these steps at any age. And often you build up some resilience by trying all sorts of different things first.

Did the Colonel say to himself "Right then, I'm gonna set up the service station to sell fried chicken and in three months I'm gonna have a global franchise business"? No, of course he didn't. He might have had big dreams, but still he started with something small and grew it—and then there was a tipping point.

Does it matter that he was in his 40s, 50s, 60s, or 70s when any of these things happened? Nope.

I'll say it again. Stop fighting for age as a limitation. It is a number.

If it helps, think about this:

Perhaps the best time to do the thing you want to do is now after all?

Perhaps when you were younger you lacked the core knowledge, maturity, ideas, network, flexibility, savings, encouragement, skills, or vision...that you have now.

How can you leverage the experience and expertise gained in your niche to serve and benefit potential customers (and give you an income)?

What do you know that no-one else knows like you know it? Go back over your responses to Task 3. And if you haven't done Task 3 yet, do it now.

SUMMARY AND ACTION POINTS:

- There is never a good time. So there's never a better time than now.
- What's your '60 per cent ready'? And what do you need to do to go from there to taking the step?
- Develop a simple one-pager. A PDF. Or just a LinkedIn post that demonstrates your knowledge. Give it to the world and see what happens. If the answer is nothing, then you've succeeded in not breaking anything. So go again.
- What do you know that no one else knows like you know it?

CHAPTER 7

YOU DON'T HAVE ENOUGH MONEY.

Money. If you treat it with respect and don't idolise it for the sake of itself, you should be OK.

But most people don't have a great relationship with money. They spend everything they earn (or more), and don't make any regular savings. Budgeting and financial acumen take a lower position in the school curriculum than quadratic equations.

Throw in observed financial habits of our parents, brand-based shopping, and over-reaching lifestyles fuelled by peer pressure and that of social media, and it's easy to see how we might be conditioned to believe we don't have enough money to make a break from traditional employment.

So this chapter will go into some detail on all these topics, challenge your thinking, and give you some practical tools and ideas to help you move in the right direction.

WHAT IS 'ENOUGH'?

The psychology of money is complex, and I don't want to attempt to get deep into it here, except to ask you, what is 'enough'?

What is enough to cover the basics, get you out of a hole, or give you a certain lifestyle? That lifestyle might include a newer car, regular holidays, *fancier* holidays. The odd takeaway or meal out. I don't know. Butler service?

Perhaps you'd like enough to be able to keep things ticking along while you do some charity work. Or support the local community or your wider family. Or save for your retirement. Or enable you to work part-time or for blocks of the year, taking what author Tim Ferris, in his book *The 4-Hour Work Week*, calls "mini-retirements". You could actually live your life now, instead of waiting until you're old and societal norms say you can kick back.

ARE SAVINGS THE BE-ALL AND END-ALL?

While savings are important, they play a different role depending on the type of going-it-alone work you do or want to do. Let's consider becoming a solopreneur/knowledge worker or a contractor.

CREATE TO SAVE

Want to sell your skills and knowledge through consulting gigs, webinars and seminars, public speaking, authoring, or one-to-one or group work? There is absolutely no reason why a lack of savings should stop you from getting started.

The term 'side hustle' has been popularised in recent years, and I saw its rise in use in the run up to and during the pandemic. It was coined in 1950s America when the Pittsburgh Courier wrote a story about a Scoutmaster with a sideline of being a prophet—for money. This psychic routine was termed a side hustle by the paper, using the 'side' bit to somehow legitimise a word you'd otherwise connect with con artistry.

Your wares could be developed entirely outside of work time. Examples include write-once-and-sell-many-times guides, PDFs, eBooks, templates, forms, 1-hour consulting sessions, or in my case redrafted CVs. You can sell them at a low cost to you on sites like **Gumroad.com**, and market them on LinkedIn.

One of my clients is sufficiently qualified in his area of expertise to occasionally be called as an expert witness. He used to do this alongside his employed work, writing reports in the evenings and weekends. Now, being free from the shackles of his employer, he can explore more opportunities for this quite lucrative line of work as part of a portfolio of services he offers.

While still employed, you can build a presence and, importantly, an additional income. An income you can put in a different bank account. One you don't touch, but that you can access if and when you need to.

Like if and when you have a bit of a dry month, so you can pay your mortgage or rent or bills. Which will most likely happen. And that's OK. It's expected, actually. You need to prepare yourself for that.

Importantly, building a cash buffer will also start to give you the confidence and backing that you'll be OK when your side hustle becomes successful enough to ditch your job.

SAVING

Some people are frugal as can be and save, save, save. They have investments and ISAs and all that stuff. Others either haven't thought about it or struggle to make ends meet as it is.

When you ask someone what they'd do if they won the lottery or one of those radio show cash prizes for picking up the phone and saying the right words, they'll probably say "treat the family to a holiday!" or "buy a new car".

You don't often hear them say: "I'm going to stick it in an ISA, high-interest bank account, or an investment fund, and let the interest compound while adding a small amount to it on a monthly basis, so in 20 years I have a really nice nest egg." Or: "Amazing, this means I can start my freelancing business without worrying about my bills for a few months!"

I'm sorry to say this, but your chances of winning either the lottery or your radio show cash prize are slim. If you want to have the certainty that you can cover your bills for a length of time whilst not receiving a regular salary, you *need* to have a fall back.

Everyone's financial situation is different, but we all have the opportunity to start saving. Even it's a small amount. At the time of writing this (2024), interest rates in the UK are the highest they have been for decades, so saving quickly has never been more attractive.

Regardless of whether you're thinking of going out on your own, putting money away for when you need it most is just sound common sense.

If you haven't already, you could start saving into a high-interest account with just a few pounds or whatever you can put away without needing it immediately. Set up a standing order from your regular bank account so it comes out as soon as you get paid. Skim it off the top. If that's difficult, imagine the income tax rate went up and you had no choice but to take a net pay cut.

Taxes go to the government to fund services. What I'm suggesting is placing your own tax on your income to help you fund your future plans. There are plenty of other resources out there (like *Money: Master the Game* by Tony Robbins) to help you with investments if you want to go down that route and make your money work even harder for you.

I've just suggested you grow your savings pot from a standing order the moment you get paid.

"But Phil, I don't have anything left at the end of the month as it is!"

Well, I'd encourage you to really, REALLY analyse your spending habits to find low-hanging fruit. Work out if the things you're spending your money on are more important than achieving freedom from the traditional 9-5, and the prospect of joining the solopreneur movement.

There are many ways to save money by spending differently.

BUDGETING

Too few people do this. I have a spreadsheet going back years that lists out all the standing orders (my monthly expenses) for utilities, council tax, mortgage, and whatnot.

This means I know what I expect to come out each and every month. I know that before I eat or drink anything, clothe myself, or do anything nice as a treat, I've got to earn that amount to cover the basics.

I have also estimated those annual costs that creep up on us if we're not prepared. Car and home insurance, MOT and car servicing, that sort of thing. Look at your costs last year and add in 20-30 per cent as a contingency in case of a necessary car or house repair, and this will help you to budget.

Once you have a total figure for all those basic living costs, divide it by 12 to give you the amount you need to put away each month so that when the day comes and the car insurance comes up, you can cover it in one go.

Now you have a monthly figure, add that on to your base expenses and you'll know what you need to cover.

Your new savings account will most likely let you set up virtual 'pots' for different types of savings or savings goals. Paying monthly for your insurance is more expensive than paying it off annually. Wouldn't it be better to save the money in advance, or at least some of it, so that when the bill comes it's not sending you into overdraft, or worse still to the credit card? Don't forget, you'll also get interest on those savings.

While I'm talking about this, I really recommend taking a look at your suppliers for all these different things. There are many ways of assessing whether you're getting the best deal for your circumstances on insurances, utilities, broadband etc.

Martin Lewis's **MoneySavingExpert.com** is a great place to start, and you'll also be able to find impartial information about savings accounts, zero per cent credit card balance transfers, and all manner of ways to make your money go further.

Have you inadvertently gone onto your mortgage provider's variable rate? If you have, get on to a fixed-rate deal and save yourself pounds every month AND over the life of your mortgage.

Once you've worked out all these numbers, you know what you've got left for feeding and clothing yourself.

I've included a budgeting tool on the next page to help you. You can download a digital version (with automations) via **the QR code at the end of the chapter**.

I said earlier that your relationship with money will be particular to you, and it is the subject of much psychological research and debate. But I can tell you one thing: it's only useful having money if you do good with it.

And that doesn't include spending it for the sake of it, or buying things you don't really need to impress your mates. Though let's face it, we've all done it.

I'm not going to say here that if you stop buying a skinny-mocha-chocca-latte each day from Costa, and start making a packed lunch, that it'll revolutionise your cash flow any more than it'll help you get save for a house deposit during a cost of living crisis. However, objectively checking your spending habits as a whole will help you shine a light on opportunities to make sensible savings that really can add up.

YOUR SUPERMARKET TROLLEY

Just observe yourself while you're shopping.

Do you fill it with the 'leading brand'? It's also the most expensive. Why not try going down a brand, maybe to the supermarket's own brand?

Do you buy lots of pre-packed convenience foods? Pricey.

Do you ever think about (or calculate) the cost per kilo of the 'family pack' versus the normal pack? Hint: they aren't always better value.

	TODAY	TARGET 1 (REDUCED/ MINDFUL SPENDING)	TARGET 2 (INCREASED SIDE EARNINGS)
Income	**£ amount (monthly)**	**£ amount (monthly)**	**£ amount (monthly)**
Salary			
Side income 1			
Side income 2			
Total monthly income (after tax, FIGURE A)	0	0	0

OPPORTUNITIES TO GROW THIS? ←

Expense	**£ amount (monthly)**	**£ amount (monthly)**	**£ amount (monthly)**
Mortgage/rent			
Gas			
Electricity			
Water			
TV/broadband			
Phone/mobile phone			
Council tax			
Car payments			
Credit card payments			
Loan repayments			
Food shopping			
Clothes/make up/lifestyle items			
Takeaways			
Nights/meals out			
Kid's clubs/activities			
Food/coffees at work			
What else?			
What else?			
What else?			
What else?			
Total base expenses (FIGURE B)	0	0	0

OPPORTUNITIES TO REDUCE THIS? ←

Review your bank statements. Where's your money going?

Review suppliers, consolidate credit cards, challenge day to day spending

How are you sabotaging your savings efforts?

Annual Expenses	**£ amount**	**£ amount**	**£ amount**
Car insurance			
Home insurance			
Car MOT			
Car tax			
Car repairs (contingency)			
Home repairs (contingency)			
Holiday savings			
Tax bill (contingency)			
Total annual expenses (FIGURE C)	0	0	0
Divide by 12 to get a monthly saving figure (FIGURE D)	0	0	0

Total monthly expenses (FIGURE B + D)	0	0	0

MINIMISE THIS

Potential monthly savings	0	0	0

MAXIMISE THIS

Potential annual savings	0	0	0

Do you regularly find you buy food and throw it away? Wasteful.

Do you live on expensive takeaways and meals out?

Do you ever do a meal plan for the week, and just buy the items you need—or buy what catches your eye and then wonder how you're going to make a meal out of it?

Do you cook from scratch? If not, what are you afraid of? Some of the simplest and cheapest things to cook are pasta sauces. Just Google a recipe if you're not sure. Even better, batch cook a load of sauce and freeze it for use another time.

"But Phil, I just don't have time to cook properly!" If you can find just one hour a week you can batch cook enough dishes to have one night a week covered for the next month (or two) with no problem at all.

If anything it will *save* you time, and be healthier and less expensive than a jar of sauce thrown over your pasta or getting a Deliveroo. Just ask yourself what the *real* excuse is for not doing these things, and then you can do something about it. Is it more important than freedom from employment?

YOUR WARDROBE

Do you go out and buy clothes and shoes and other lifestyle items on a whim? Or do you look to see where you could get the best items you can afford at the most reasonable price?

Is your wardrobe full of stuff you've never worn? Why not sell it on **Vinted**? It really is easy.

Do you always buy branded gear for you and the kids? Is it necessary? Who are you trying to impress? Try going for a quality unbranded t-shirt over one with 'BOSS' emblazoned on it.

Did you know that the wealthiest people in the world don't tend to wear clothes with luxury brand names all over them? They generally don't feel the need to impress their mates. Want to be wealthy? Then *think* and *act wealthy*.

YOUR LIFESTYLE HABITS

Do you have a gym membership you don't use? Either start using it or cancel the payment.

Do you buy a new toy for your kids every week? They don't need all that stuff. Honestly, they don't. Do you cave in to pester power for the brightly coloured Peppa Pig comic and the crappy plastic toy that costs a fiver? Say no! They might throw a hissy fit, but they'll get over it.

Do you pour money into eating convenience lunches and buying coffees while you're at work? Try making a sandwich or a salad (boil a few eggs and take one with your salad each day) and taking a bottle of water (aka the packed lunch). Or take last night's leftovers.

You'll save £5-10 a day MINIMUM just by doing that. That could be £200 you're saving for an outlay of around £20 worth of ingredients over the course of a month. That's £2,400 a year, right there.

And please don't tell me you don't have enough time to make a sandwich. I'll hit the bullshit button immediately. What do you want more, the convenience of being able to grab a focaccia or a Maccies while you're at work, or being able to ditch 'work' in its traditional sense? Make five minutes in the morning. Get up earlier. Or do it the night before.

If you don't believe you have the capacity to save (or haven't done anything about it before), looking at your budget, shopping trolley, wardrobe, and lifestyle should give you some ideas to get you started.

I'm not saying this is a silver bullet, but it is about mindset, challenging your excuses and assumptions, encouraging objective analysis, and in some cases, making tough calls on what's more important to you.

If you could save two and a half grand just from changing your shopping/eating habits, think about what you could save if you properly looked at your budget.

Just challenge yourself to take a look. See where the opportunities are.

All my life I've seen people living to or beyond their means. When a pay rise comes, they spend it, not save it. You don't have to be that person.

So, please ask yourself: "When I say I've not got enough savings, am I using it as an excuse for not taking action and just getting on with it?"

Because in the future when you look back, regardless of whether it works, you'll have taken the steps required to go out on your own and follow your dream.

TASK 5—CONTROL YOUR CASH.

Take a proper look at your finances.

Use the monthly budget calculator to work out where your money is going right now. Where are the surprises?

Where could (or should) you cut back?

Could you shift your credit card debt to a zero per cent balance transfer card?

Could you challenge yourself to try some different, lower-cost brands?

Do the kids need a different paid activity every night?

Are you spending more on takeaways and nights out than you thought?

If a new, lower income was necessary, how much could you cut back by? So what could you afford to put into a separate pot?

How much do you realistically need to earn to meet that new budget?

Just how important to you is making this change in your life?

SUMMARY AND ACTION POINTS:

- You don't need to quit your job to start something on the side.
- Consider making a name for yourself in your chosen side hustle before handing in your notice.
- If you're already free of the corporate world—just get going! You've got absolutely nothing in your way.
- Find ways to assess your real-world spending. What can you live without?[6]

NOTE—this does not constitute financial advice, but it is a set of ideas you may apply or tailor to your own circumstances.

---

6 A client of mine was contemplating hiring me for a year to coach and support him in a few areas of his life. However my fee, in his words, was "more than my car payments" and he didn't consider it affordable. And that's cool, it just means he was, at that time, putting his car (and whatever that brought with it) ahead of his own development and getting to where he wanted to get to more quickly. He had all sorts of options to remain mobile *and* take up my services. He chose, consciously or unconsciously, how and where to spend his money.

SCAN THE QR CODE ABOVE
FOR MY FREE BUDGETING TOOL.

ARE THE THINGS YOU'RE SPENDING MONEY ON TODAY MORE IMPORTANT THAN FREEDOM FROM THE 9-5 TOMORROW?

CHAPTER 8

THINKING BIG IS GETTING IN YOUR WAY.

"I'd love to go out on my own" she said. "But I..."

Adam was on a weekend break with his family, the kind in a woodland where every amenity is catered for. Shops, restaurants, spa, pool, waterslides, crazy golf, zip wires. All that. Adam is my coach.

He was having a massage while his kids were in the waterpark. As often happens, conversation with the masseuse flowed and it turned to her desire to work for herself as a beauty therapist.

Out came a list of 'reasons' why she didn't think she could.

She said that she lacked premises, a wide enough customer base, a website, a dedicated work phone, a Facebook page...and so on.

As far as she was concerned, she needed all these things ready and in place before she could do someone's nails and charge them for it.

"Start smaller than you think," Adam said.

She didn't quite understand.

"Well, you're saying that you need premises, lots of customers, a website, a dedicated work phone, a Facebook page and all that—and then you can start your side-business?"

"Yes."

"What do you really need? If you had to start the business tomorrow, what would you *really* need?"

"Er..."

"Do you have the main equipment—I'm guessing polishes, files, a light?"

"Yes."

"Do you have a few people you know who would love you to paint their nails that would be happy to pay you the going rate (not mates rates)?"

"Yes."

"Could you do this either from home or go to them?"

And then an inflatable donut-sized penny dropped like a family of waterslide riders into a plunge pool.

She didn't need a website. Or premises. Or a Facebook page. Or any of the other things she thought she needed. She already had the very basics. And from there she could start, and then grow. Serve a handful of people. Ask for a review—on Facebook, Google, or Trustpilot. They're free.

She could ask for referrals by simply saying: "Who do you know who might like their nails to look like that before a big event? Will you give them my number?"

And so it goes. Start smaller than you think. Then notch it down one more step and you might surprise yourself with what you can achieve.

The thing about that big list of things she thought she needed? She put the list in the way of just doing the thing.

Those limitations or excuses you're making for yourself as to why you can't possibly do the thing you want to do, they are just getting in the way. In fact, you're getting in your own way.

You're letting made-up limitations and fears get in the way of you taking the smallest of steps. Then you're standing there in their corner of the ring, tooled up and fighting for them. And not only fighting for them, but inflating them so they seem more important or more challenging than they really are.

I can almost see you there with an industrial pump, with its hose shoved into the backside of your excuses, happily blowing air into them until they look like the Stay-Puft Marshmallow Man from *Ghostbusters*, treading through the streets and walking all over your dreams.

You've probably had the conversation with someone already.

"I'd really like to go out on my own but...[insert list of limitations you've sat on for years]."

Well, here I am knocking on your front door and shouting "Bullshit!"

Stop fighting for your limitations and look at what you already have.

What's the bare minimum of what you might need?

Look, I've been there. That's how I know.

When I started out in 2020, the second time around, and this time not as a contractor but as a bona fide knowledge worker, I did start small. Out of necessity.

Here's what I didn't have:

- a guaranteed income;
- a fancy garden office;
- 10,000 LinkedIn followers;
- ready and waiting customers;
- a newsletter with 2,000 subscribers;
- a podcast channel, lighting, and microphones;
- any real knowledge of running a B2C business;
- people telling me "You should go out on your own";
- expectations that I could turn enough revenue to become full-time.

What I did have:

- time,
- Google,
- a six-year old laptop,
- a five-year old phone,
- savings for a few months,
- moral support from my partner,
- desire to help people live better lives,
- a bit of gumption, but not a lot of conviction,
- hunger to do something different with my life,
- 2,000 LinkedIn followers I'd built up over 13 years,
- 25 years' knowledge of what a decent CV looked like,
- a small spare room I'd already turned into an office (you don't need one of these, I was fortunate).

I tried not to let the things in the first list get in my way.

The easiest and quickest way I found to sell my knowledge was on **PeoplePerHour** (**Fiverr** and **Upwork** are similar alternatives). Simples. And I used it for as long as I needed to until people came to me through LinkedIn.

But for you the channels might be different.

You might know loads of people on Facebook that you can message or write a post to. Or you coule create a Facebook business page.

Putting a card up in the local supermarket might be the right step.

What's the smallest thing you can do?

The *biggest* thing you can do is stop fighting for your limitations and consider what you already have.

TASK 6—WHAT DO YOU ALREADY HAVE?

Write your own list of the things you think you need to get going. Then another list of the things you already have.

If I told you that you HAD to start offering a service tomorrow or I'd go all *Taken* and kidnap your family, how would you do it with what you already have?

SUMMARY AND ACTION POINTS:

- Thinking big is OK, but start smaller than you think.
- Make a list of all the things you think you need to get going. Then ask yourself—if I HAD to start this business tomorrow, what could I get away with not having in place?
- Get creative. Have some fun coming up with ideas (or researching tools) that cost you no money to use.
- It's fine to to make some mistakes along the way. It means you're growing.

SIMPLE FREE ONLINE TOOLS:

FIVERR, UPWORK, PEOPLEPERHOUR

Finding gigs/individual pieces of work. Build your profile and publicise your offers. Screen grab client feedback and use it in your marketing.

LINKEDIN, FACEBOOK, INSTAGRAM

You know where your audience is. Try not to do everything at once. Focus on frequency and regularity on one platform before trying to work on another.

TRUSTPILOT

I was late to this party, but I asked all my earlier clients if they would write a review for me to help build my profile. At the time of writing, I have 60 five-star reviews on Trustpilot and prospective clients are finding me through it too. It's become an invaluable (and free) channel.

CANVA

Designing social media posts, banners, documents—the world is your oyster. I use the pro version but there's so much for a beginner in the free version.

STOP FIGHTING FOR YOUR LIMITATIONS AND CONSIDER WHAT YOU ALREADY HAVE.

PART 2

WHAT WOULD I SELL, AND WHO WOULD BUY ANYTHING FROM ME ANYWAY?

WORKING OUT YOUR 'THING' CAN BE HARD.

And imposter syndrome will tell us that even if we come up with something, no one will want to buy it.

So what's the point?

Well, that's why you're reading this book. Part 2 will help you think about the kinds of problems you solve for people. Or could solve. Because sat in those problems are solutions that people are willing to pay money for.

And they are problems you've solved before. It could be the advice and guidance you'd give someone doing what you do—but with few years less experience.

Consider this very book. Do I know everything about working for yourself? No! But I know enough, and I know more than you, which is why you're happy for me to teach you.

"That's all very well Phil, but where are all these people I can sell to?"

It's a big world out there, shrunk by technology. I now regularly work with clients on every continent, because it's easy to. I'll go into using LinkedIn in quite a bit of depth to help with this.

Let's not forget the importance of word-of-mouth. News of great customer experiences can spread like wildfire, so I'll be talking about that too.

And finally, I'll take you through the often overlooked slow-burner that is just simply being a decent person. Though I've called the chapter "Don't be a dick".

CHAPTER 9

WHAT PROBLEMS DO YOU SOLVE, AND FOR WHOM?

Before I worked for Amazon, I tried contracting and for a while it was ideal for me, but then something changed. I felt like I was on a bit of a boom-bust cycle, neck-deep in a contract for six months, then it'd finish and I'd come up for air and it'd feel like the world had moved on. I was so focused on each project that I almost forgot the outside world. I lost track of time.

As a contractor, you're there to solve whatever problem the company is facing. Or you're there to deliver an outcome—and they don't know about the problems yet.

They don't want to take on someone permanently to deliver this piece of work (which could be time-limited, like a maternity cover contract) so they'll happily pay someone a bit more than they would normally pay a permy to come in, do the job, and get out again without too much fuss.

I still know many people who are 'career interims' in so far as they haven't had a permanent job in years. They spend their time happily swinging from contract to contract like Tarzan in the trees, leading projects and programmes, fixing problems, and charging day rates through their limited company. And they still love it. It's interesting, lucrative, and you get to meet a lot of people and learn more (and more quickly) than in any permanent role.

Upon leaving Amazon, I decided I absolutely did not want to go back to working for another corporate—with a boss, politics, a salary, performance reviews and all the stuff that went with it.

I also knew I didn't want to go contracting again, and even the idea of it at the time was far too stressful to give airtime.

I'd been watching many of Simon Sinek's videos, including his *Start with Why* TedTalk. If you've not heard of it, Google it—it really helped me at the time, even if some the analysis he proffers is perhaps a bit flawed.

The basic principle is that most businesses start with 'what'—what do they do/sell/manufacture. Like Dell, in Sinek's example: "We make computers."

Businesses then progress to 'how'. The how might be "using high end componentry, research, and manufacturing facilities".

Then to 'why'. Why did they go into business? Because they thought they could make money by selling computers.

The Sinek take is to reverse this thinking, with the 'why' representing some higher purpose other than to make money.

Sinek suggests companies like Amazon and Apple started with their 'why', such as "we're the Earth's most customer-centric company", and innovated from there. And this meant they could become more flexible in what they sell, as people are bought into the brand, not the product[7].

I still have the piece of flip chart paper (somewhere) on which I started deeply contemplating what I could do instead of the job I was doing. There were some key themes for me that played to my strengths.

---

7 There is a counter argument of course—did Jeff Bezos really sit in his garage thinking "I want to create the most customer-centric company in the world" or did he think "I want to capitalise on this thing called the internet. What can I sell? I know, books." He wasn't thinking of a higher purpose, he just had FOMO about growing old and regretting not doing something cool with the new technology.

I wanted to do something where I could:

- help people live better lives,
- use some of my creative skills,
- engage in short-turnaround projects,
- work with people one-to-one or in small groups,
- play to my strengths around careers and recruitment,
- gain positive validation quickly to rebuild my confidence.

Some of those things are 'whys' and others are 'hows'. I wasn't too prescriptive in using the model, other than as a launch pad for my thinking. I just wanted to live a more authentic life, doing more stuff I enjoyed with people I liked, working in my Zone of Genius with a decent amount of variety, and getting paid for the privilege.

Then I came to the 'what'. What was my particular set of skills? Where could I add value without trying very hard, and earn money, whilst living by my 'why'? What would people pay for? And what *didn't* I like doing, and what environments did I want to avoid?

I had inadvertently modelled my own version of Ikigai (pronounced ick-ee-guy)—the Japanese concept meaning 'a reason for being'. It encourages you to think about what you love, what the world needs, what you're good at, and what you can get paid for. At the centre of this fairly complex Venn diagram you'll find your Ikigai.

My answer was CV writing and career coaching, though the latter would come later—or rather, I would later realise that coaching was what I was actually doing.

I'd learned that I didn't like the all-in or all-out nature of contracting, and I preferred much shorter (and perhaps more intense) pieces of work, where I could get in and out, and get fast positive feedback (and the dopamine hit).

I knew I was good at writing, asking questions, and refining complex responses and bits of information into easy-to-consume text. And, I enjoyed doing all

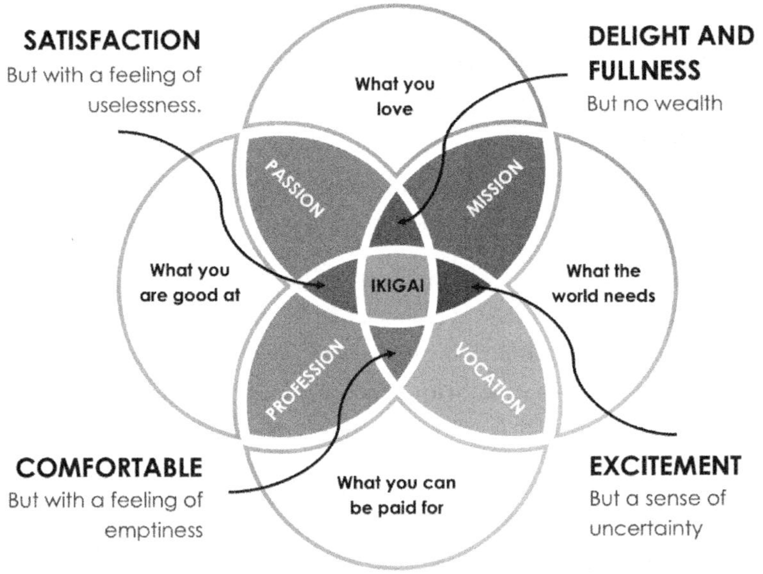

these things, but most of all I enjoyed helping people make sense of their careers and finding the thread that for so many is missing. I knew their problems.

As a recruiter, I knew the huge volume of CVs I'd seen were pretty poor. I knew I could add value easily and help people get shortlisted. The world needed this.

After doing some basic research, I found there were a handful of 'CV writing' companies. They seemed expensive and faceless, low in personality, and lacking a personal touch.

I discovered many, many, CV writers on the freelancer marketplaces, some charging very little, and others what I considered to be a lot (at the time). Some with recruitment backgrounds, some with operational leadership backgrounds, others with HR backgrounds. I had all three.

Ikigai is a great tool, and I'd encourage you to use it to get you thinking about what you can do with your life to live as your authentic self. But the 'what you can be paid for' bit is crucial.

Depending on the standard of living you want to achieve (and remembering I've talked a lot in this book already about what is 'enough') you must remember that whatever you do, it needs to pay—otherwise it's simply a hobby.

It needs to pay for more than your time. Exchanging your time for money might be where you start, but finding a way to add value and generate a profit should be where you aim. It took me a while to switch my thinking around, but now I sell based on the value I can generate for my clients, not how long it takes me to do it.

Whilst I started with my 'why' of helping other people live better lives, I found myself charging a low fee for the work I was doing, and thinking about it in terms of an hourly rate.

When I realised I should be pricing based on the *value* I was providing and the *problem* I was solving for my customers (that is, 'value-based pricing'), everything changed. I changed my marketing approach from selling a CV writing service to focusing on the outcomes for the customer. I started asking myself what problems I was solving and for whom.

In 2002, I attended Dale Carnegie's sales school, where I was introduced to the concept of the 'Dominant Buying Motive'. No one buys the thing for the sake of buying the thing; they buy the thing because it helps them fulfil a deeper want or need, and you can trace those needs back to Maslow's Hierarchy of Needs.

A job seeker doesn't buy a CV writing service because they just want a new CV to save on their computer. It has zero intrinsic value. It's what they can *do* with it. Job seekers' high-level problems include:

- not getting any interviews,
- not hearing back from applications sent.

Peel back the onion. Why would these things be a problem?

- I want a new job because I'm sick of my boss/the commute/pay etc.

- I've lost my job.
- I hate the culture of presenteeism.
- I'm bored and want a new challenge.
- I'm used to being approached for jobs, but that's not happening.

Go again. What's at the root of the problem?

- My job is affecting my health.
- I'm not seeing my family or friends.
- I don't feel like me when I'm at work and life's too short.
- I want to do something more challenging.
- I deserve to earn more.
- I really like fancy cars and I have a big mortgage so want more money.
- I just want to be happy in what I'm doing for eight hours a day.

You can do this exercise in conjunction with the Ikigai one. Come up with a list of things you can do, you enjoy, the world needs, and people will pay for—and then for each one write another list of the problems faced by the people who might buy it. Not just at a transactional level, but more deeply.

It's these things that will become the levers you'll pull when you come to promote what you're doing. For centuries advertising has focused on the features and benefits of products. These days, focusing on specific problems or pain points your potential customers have (and how you can take the pain away) is a great way of connecting with the buyer on an emotional level. There's more on solving customer problems in the next chapter.

In the context of a CV Writer and Careers Coach, my clients might want a promotion, or a new job in a different company that pays them 30 per cent more.

But the problem behind that problem might be that they want to be at home more to spend quality time with their partner, kids, or friends. Or maybe they're struggling to pay their mortgage or have their desired lifestyle.

My take is that having a clearer understanding of their value and what they're good at (and enjoy doing)—showcased in an effective CV—will help them resolve those pain points.

So I worked out the different levers I could pull from my knowledge of working in recruitment and from being an applicant myself.

You'll remember I said earlier in the book that I dislike selling. But selling doesn't feel like selling when you're asking people questions, uncovering their problems and goals, and helping them see that the thing you do will help them solve it, or relieve the pain.

They want to know that you understand their pain and that you can take it away. Imagine your offer is the paracetamol for their challenge.

You've seen Dragon's Den, right? How many times have you seen someone come on with a new product they've slaved over, and the Dragons don't buy in because the 'problem' the product is selling simply isn't great enough to warrant the 'solution'.

So go to town on listing out not just the problem singular you solve at the surface, but the problem underneath that, and the problem underneath that. Then you get close to finding out how you can market what you're doing.

Saving people time and money or thinking about how you can make someone's life easier are great starting points to work outwards from.

Once you get going, you might find you have several different products or services, or even audiences, depending on which bit of your expertise you want to pull on.

One of my clients does high-fee work that is infrequent, middle-ranking fee work that he gets more of, and lower-paid gigs that give back in some way—the nice-to-do work. It's a great mixture to have. But when you're starting out, try focusing on doing (and marketing) just one service for 90 days. Get known for solving that particular problem.

SUMMARY AND ACTION POINTS:

- Find out what your potential clients' pain points are. Research them, ask questions, run LinkedIn polls, use your own experience. How can you help them and make their lives easier?
- What's your 'why'?
- Spend some time considering your Ikigai. Make sure the answer pays, otherwise it's just a hobby.

GET KNOWN FOR SOLVING THAT PARTICULAR PROBLEM.

CHAPTER 10

LINKEDIN IS YOUR FRIEND.

"I don't know enough people to sell to."

Well, you don't *need* to know them *just yet*.

Back in the day (when it was launched in 2003), LinkedIn was considered the 'professional networking site', creating a space where businesspeople could exchange virtual business cards and network like they were at a conference.

It was the place where you'd display your career profile (effectively your CV) and apply for jobs or hope employers would approach you.

It was stuffy. The anti-Facebook. Definitely not MySpace, but a kind of Friends Reunited for work. Not the place for pictures of your holidays, cars, dinners, sunset views, and cats falling off televisions.

As time has progressed it has become altogether more relaxed. Sure, there's still a proportion of the users who live in the late 2000s world, wear a shirt and tie or heels every day, and consider it a professional networking site where there's no place for 'personal' posts.

The pandemic changed everything big-time. We started letting our work colleagues into our homes every day on Zoom and Teams calls. Were we in our work gear? No, we were in our hoodies. Were we in polished shoes? No. Quite possibly under the desk we were in pyjamas and slippers. Or less.

Things started to become necessarily more relaxed. People started posting more personal posts. Selfies crept in. 'No makeup' selfies. In-their-PJs selfies.

Eating-homemade-sandwich selfies. Pictures of their desks. Their gardens. Their pets.

Slowly, people learned they could leverage this more personal approach to networking. Solopreneurs started turning up daily, providing free advice explaining everything you need to do in order to do the thing you want to do. Zeroing in on the precise problem you have in your business and sharing ideas on how to solve it.

Now LinkedIn is awash with creators telling you how to write interesting and engaging posts based on personality and solving problems.

Why are they doing this? Giving all this knowledge away for free? It's madness, right?
Wrong.

Any business is in the trust business. We say people buy from people, but what we mean is people buy from people they trust. And how better to foster trust with complete strangers than to tell them, for free, how they can solve their problems? Sounds counter intuitive, doesn't it?

In the old days, you just had to advertise something with a catchy strapline and give the impression that if they bought that thing they'd either save money or time, impress their friends, or look more attractive.

Think of the Snickers bar. In the 80s it was called a Marathon in the UK, and the adverts focused on what it was: chocolate, nuts, caramel, nougat. Now? Mars' advertising teams bring to your attention that when you're hungry, you can lose the plot a bit. "You're not yourself when you're hungry—grab a Snickers". Snickers now becomes the solution to the problem of hunger impacting your ability to make decisions (or just be reasonable!).

The knowledge worker industry is predicated on sharing enough information and tools for free that you'll either go off and do the thing you want to do yourself, or hire the person or company that built your trust in their ability to do it for you.

Some people will, without doubt, do it themselves. They just need a gentle push in the right direction, a couple of tools or ideas to get them over the starting line, and they're off. And that's cool too. It's cool because you've provided them with that shove, and regardless of whether they ever tell you, they might tell someone else to check you out.

So what if they've not paid you any money for that knowledge? Consider it free advertising.

And anyway, some won't go down the DIY route. They'll get as far as they can with the free stuff you've provided them with—knowledge, templates, guides, ideas—and come to you anyway.

Plenty of my paying clients are living proof of this journey.

"Phil, I've been following and reading your content, applying what you've been telling me, but I'm not quite happy with what I've done—can you help?"

Sure. Then we have a conversation to understand their needs and problems. What's getting in their way? "OK, well there's a couple of main ways you can work with me to handle *x*, *y* and *z*." And a client, sometimes, is born.

So, that LinkedIn profile of yours. You know, the one with the company's logo and mission statement screenshotted and used as your banner image? Or no banner image at all?

And with your job title and company name as the headline?

And some blurb about each company you've worked for in the experience section?

Ditch it.

I'm not here to shame you; I'm here to tell you what works. And up until now, you've being doing the best you can with the tools and knowledge (and mindset) you have. And that's fine.

But, if you wish to become a service provider selling what you know, building a personal brand and reputation on LinkedIn is about the simplest, cheapest, and most effective thing you can do. So it needs to count.

Getting your house in order on LinkedIn is a must. At the time of writing, LinkedIn has 875 million users, so here are some tips on how to get going quickly and get the basics in place so that you get yourself in front of some of those eyeballs.

REPLACE YOUR PROFILE PICTURE

Is your picture from 2003 when LinkedIn first launched, with you in a suit and either a Jennifer Aniston haircut or directional facial hair? Or both? Or the one from that wedding with a drink in your hand? Or with your arm around a friend? Or on holiday somewhere?

Get rid of that and just get someone to take a few shots of you outside in semi-relaxed gear. For me that's a flannel shirt or a Guns n' Roses or Metallica t-shirt, because that's how I turn up for work, wherever I'm working and whomever I'm working with. It's not over corporate. Just make sure it's well-lit from the front. No glare. Flattish light (so not in scorching sunshine). Ideally, get someone else to take it on your phone, rather than a selfie.

Go to **remove.bg** in your browser, upload the photo, and choose a coloured background. It's like magic. Download the new image, save it, and upload it back in to LinkedIn.

Done.

If you don't have a profile picture or for some reason don't want to put one up, consider this: if you have one, LinkedIn statistics report profiles with a picture receive 21 times more profile views and nine times more connection requests.

Make sure your face fills 60 per cent of the picture, it's only you in it, and use a high-resolution picture, not a zoomed-in grainy one. And smile. Laugh, even. Show a bit of 'you'. A study of 800 profile pictures found that a smile showing teeth was rated twice as 'likeable' than one with a closed-mouth smile. And likeablility builds trust, clicks, and potential clients.

WRITE A NEW HEADLINE

Get rid of the job title and employer name (the LinkedIn default). Instead, say what problems you solve and for whom. Your headline is the only bit of your profile (along with your picture) that'll appear in searches and above any comment you make on someone else's post. So tell people what you can do for them, and quickly.

What will your target audience value the most and what will make them want to look at your profile? You need a hook: something that will get their attention, something that speaks to them and their problems.

Do you help small business owners become more efficient?

Say "*I help small business owners unlock operational efficiencies* | **[chosen sector/ niche]** *by* **[how you do it.]**"

Do you help FTSE100 businesses unlock efficiencies and new multi-million-pound revenue streams? Say that.

[Job specialism] | *Helping* **[ideal client][resolve *x* problem]** *through* **[*x* solution]**| **[*x* skill one, *x* skill two]**

or

[Job specialism] | *Helping* **[ideal client] [do *x*] [without the *y*]**

MAKE THE 'ABOUT' SECTION ABOUT THEM, NOT YOU

Write the About section like you're talking directly to your target customer. That is, in terms of 'you'—that is the customer/reader—not 'I'.

The reader doesn't care what you do; they care about their own problems. So help them remember what their problems are and then tell them what you can do (and have done) about it. Use this simple PAPS model:

Problem
Agitate
Proof
Solution

This piece-of-cake method enables you to focus most on the pain points or problems your ideal customers are having, amplify the issue (or stir it up/agitate it) so that they feel like they've got to do something about it, and then provide a way to get rid of the pain—this is the solution.

To get this right, you need to understand more about your potential customers' problems. Consider talking to them. Asking them questions. Listening to the responses. Finding out why it's a problem. Then you'll know how to speak to them in language they understand about their own problems.

Once you've agitated the problem further, you can emerge like a knight on a white horse with a solution.

Make this more powerful by inserting proof or validation around your experience. If you have directly comparable experience from your traditional work life, use it. Tell the story: *x* person was struggling to resolve *y* problem, and with *z* help, they achieved *x*.

Try adding a CTA (call to action) at the end to spur them to get in touch, go to your website, or request some guide or document you want them to gift them. But make it about them. So not "Download my LinkedIn Success PDF here", but more "Gain New Customers Fast With These 3 LinkedIn Tips". Or whatever is appropriate for you.

Here's an example:

Owners of small businesses tell me that keeping track of their finances is a night-

mare. [**The Problem**]

Particularly towards year end, when they haven't a clue how much revenue they've brought in, how much they should pay themselves in dividends, and more to the point, how to minimise their tax liabilities. [**Agitate**]

With 25 years of helping small businesses like yours keep control of their numbers and retain more of their earnings [**Proof**], *I can work with you to make life simpler and richer.* [**Solution**]

Book a business finance discovery call with me and I will help you work out... [**Call to action**]

Feel free to build this out and enrich it, but the important thing is you are demonstrating that you understand your customer and their problems. So get to know them first, and don't guess.

If you've been in that sector for years and this is what you want to continue doing (but for yourself) then this should be relatively straight forward. If not, learn. LinkedIn polls are great as a quick and dirty means of market research, though there's no substitute for talking to real prospects and learning from the horses' mouths.

GET YOUR EXPERIENCE SECTION UP TO DATE

Don't want your employer or colleagues to know you're starting a side hustle just yet? Rather than updating your headline and About section, just make sure your current and most recent jobs are aligned well to the kinds of knowledge services you want to sell.

This helps potential customers gain validation from your experience that you know what you're talking about. So use the experience section to drop in bullet points of how you've solved similar (or at least related) problems to those your customers are facing.

Make the information super clear.

Start with a line or two about why you were hired and what you were there to do—regardless of whether you realised it when you joined, like:

Engaged to [**solve *x* problem**]. *Led a team of 43 through three directors and held a £21M sales budget.*

Then, demonstrate how you added relevant value. Consider this structure:

[**Achievement**] by [**action**], which resolved [**problem**].

The achievement should preferably be numerical. A percentage improvement, money saved, income generated, process steps removed, disasters avoided.

The action is what you did to achieve the achievement. The project you led, the idea you came up with, the initiative you initiated.

Then bring it back to the problem this solved—and for whom, if it's not obvious.

Like: *Saved a client 32 per cent of their annual marketing budget and increased their return on advertising spend by 13 per cent* [**Achievement**] *by overhauling their marketing strategy and focusing on three new outdoor campaigns* [**Action**]. *This helped the business reach the new markets they failed to attract previously* [**Problem**].

And: *Grew revenues by £435K/year (17 per cent)* [**Achievement**] *by reviewing the product mix and implementing a targeted marketing campaign* [**Action**]—*enabling the business to invest in much-needed new tooling* [**Problem**].

PUT OUT A POST

I know a lot of people find this scary. But write one and hit 'post'. You might be afraid because you don't want to look daft, have someone disagree with you, or get something wrong. Perhaps you just don't see yourself as the sort of person who pokes their head above the parapet lest they should get an arrow in their eye. Or something.

But I'll let you into a secret. No one gives a fuck about what anyone else is writing, not that much anyway, because they're too busy in their own heads, and reading to reply and have their own say. So don't get too wound up about what other people think and just do it anyway.

This section is not meant to be a full guide to writing on LinkedIn, as honestly there is SO much out there to learn from other sources and by following other LinkedIn writers and creators that it would just take over this book. Search "LinkedIn ghostwriters". But here's a few ideas to get you going.

The best way I've found to create content ideas is to think about the main problem your potential customer has, and then break that down into several smaller problems, and write about those. This helps you demonstrate your authority in your field. It's OK to have an opinion. Just imagine you were advising someone face to face. Someone who has paid you for your knowledge.

With my CV writer hat on, this was my approach: Generally, a CV has four-to-six sections – from the name/contact details bit all the way down to education and hobbies. I took each one of those in turn and thought about the problems people face in getting them right. For each of those sub-problems, I had a solution—and that's what I wrote about, using that Problem-Agitate-Proof-Solution approach I mentioned earlier.

So from one main problem, "how can I write a CV that gets me noticed" I can create five categories of content, and then four to five items in each. From that one main problem I can harvest the ideas for 25 posts.

This is about providing value to your audience. Keep each post punchy, write as if your reader is 13 years old (so keep it simple) and avoid great big clumps of text, as they are difficult to read. Put a line of space between sentences to help the reader skim over your words. Spend some time on the platform and read other people's posts objectively. What were you able to read easily? What caught your attention? What didn't?

A good way of starting your post is with a 'hook'—that is the short sentence that gets the reader to take notice and read more. Here are some examples:

THE "I WISH I'D KNOWN" HOOK

3 things I wish I'd known about [**your specialism or the problem you solve**] *before* [**I took *x* action**]:

1. [**Thing 1**]
2. [**Thing 2**]
3. [**Thing 3**]

THE "WAYS TO SOLVE YOUR PROBLEM" HOOK

3 ways to improve your [**sales/profits/employee engagement (their problem)**]:

THE "HOW I..." HOOK

How I [**did something**] *that* [**achieved something**] *in* [***x* steps**]:

THE "BIGGEST MISTAKES" HOOK

The 3 biggest mistakes [**your ideal customer**] *make* [**trying to achieve *x***] *and how to get it right:*

If you're new to putting yourself out there like that, this might feel like a bit of a stretch. Uncomfortable. But guess what, you *do* have technical knowledge and expertise that other people can learn from.

Imagine you are you, but two or three years ago. What advice would you give your then-self to help make your life easier, or solve your problems?

Let me tell you, there'll be countless people out there in *exactly* that situation. So give them the real-life guidance and experience you've gained through the mistakes you've made and experiences you've had.

Write it in a Word document to start off if you want. Check it over to make sure it makes sense, helps solve the problem, and is error-free. Then hit post.

You might be surprised that only about three people see it. At the start that might be the case. It's like you've sweated over this damn thing for ages to get it right, worried about saying something someone might find controversial, and then no-one's seen it anyway.

Good, and well done—you got the first post out the way. Now do another one tomorrow. And the next day. You can build from there.

If this is too much of a stretch for your confidence, start smaller. Harness 'commenting'. Look at your feed. Find posts that mention things you have knowledge on, the things you'd advise on if you could.

Make a comment. Have an opinion. Make a statement. Ask a question. Something that shows you as an authority in that space. Make it useful, provide your insight.

Go on. Be brave. Do it.

NETWORK

Take a stroll back through your work history and find people on LinkedIn you used to work with. Managers, peers, team members, suppliers, partners, clients—internal AND external.

Put their names in the search bar or search up the company and select 'people' to find lists of people that either work there now or used to.

Do the same for client and supplier companies, if you were directly involved with them. Find the people and drop them a LinkedIn message. You might need to connect with or follow them first. Either way, (and regardless of what they are now doing in their latest role) say something like:

"Hi [**name**], it's been a really long time! How are you doing?

"A lot's happened since we were working on [**the thing**] together—I went to [***x* company**] then [***y* company**]—and now I'm going out on my own so I'm keeping an eye out for suitable [**contracts/pieces of work**].

"Would be great to catch up and find out what you've been up to—I'm trying to reignite the network."

These people are there and waiting to hear from you. You just never know what a conversation will bring. Some of the catch-up calls I've had turned into thousands of pounds' worth of work. Build your business up one conversation at a time.

SUMMARY AND ACTION POINTS:

- Update your LinkedIn profile. Focus on the problems you solve and for whom. Be specific.
- Get posting. Post content that gives value to your audience (specifically your target customer) and builds your authority.
- Comment on other people's posts. Use it as another opportunity to demonstrate authority—but don't be a knob about it.
- Find and follow content creators, copywriters, and ghostwriters. They give daily tips on how to pimp your profile and up your posting game.

YOU JUST NEVER KNOW WHAT ONE CONVERSATION WILL BRING.

CHAPTER 11
USE YOUR NETWORK AND WORD-OF-MOUTH.

Former colleagues, business partners, clients.

Hiding out in your little black book, your LinkedIn network or your phone, are the names and numbers of people you used to work with.

People you used to sit side-by-side with, have a coffee with, moan about somebody to, sell to, or buy from. Suppliers, partners, people you met at conferences.

You might surprise yourself as to just how many people you already know well in your immediate, first-hand network.

These people (assuming you got on okay with them) might not only be your future customers, but sounding boards. Confidantes. A source of referrals. They might have ideas for you that you've not considered.

I've built so much of my word-of-mouth business by just getting back in touch with people. I can think of a handful off the top of my head where a quick text, email, LinkedIn message, or (heaven forbid) a phone call led to business through referral.

If you're generally a nice person and haven't pissed too many people off in the past, these conversations and rekindlings can be a gold mine—as well as a real confidence booster. They're warm connections.

Have a catch up with someone for half an hour (or even an hour) and find out what they've been up to. They'll probably be very happy to tell you.

Ask questions. Be curious for the sake of curiosity. Learn. What have they been doing since you worked together? What projects have they been working on?

At some point they'll ask what you've been doing. Now it's your turn. You can tell them what jobs you've been in, sure, but come up with a couple of lines to summarise all that and then make a giant segue to say: "And all that's led me to where I am now, which is..." And tell them about the thing you're doing.

"I'm thinking of/putting some plans together to go out on my own/build a side business."

"About six months ago I started building a **[niche]** business/working on a plan to go out on my own."

"Oh right, cool, doing what?"

Then out comes the killer line.

You need to have worked out who you help, how you help them, and why—then say that.

Here are a few examples.

"I've always loved the great outdoors and working with my hands, and I haven't been using my creative skills in my job, so I'm setting up as a landscape gardener. I completed my **[insert relevant course]** last year and have been advising close friends and family on their gardens, and now I'm going for it and doing short projects during weekends to get going."

"I've worked out that I really love helping HR departments to reshape how they do things, and I get bored in jobs after a couple of years doing business-as-usual stuff. So I'm going solo as a contractor to lead change projects."

"I've loved working in accountancy practices and now I've got the experience of working in industry too, I've decided I want a bit more control over who I work with and how I do that—so I'm setting up my own practice."

Or, in my case:

"I realised the part of CV writing I enjoy the most is the consultation—asking the questions that help my clients work out where their real value is and what they're good at, and helping clients grow their confidence and build a game plan for their lives. So I've developed the business into an executive coaching practice."

Depending on the other person's response, this is your conversation springboard.

You could tell them about who you want to work with (or who might benefit the most from working with you), why you want to work with them, and what benefits they might get from doing so. Using the four examples I've given:

"I really want to work with mid-income clients with smallish gardens to start off with so I can quickly build a portfolio of finished work and potential referrals—and build trust within my market."

"My experience is in medium-sized businesses, 2-5,000 employees, and I've been in project teams in larger companies too, working across the business to drive change and, shape projects and get troubled initiatives back on track."

"Large companies lose hundreds of thousands (if not millions) of pounds a year through poor practice, and much of my work has been helping their operational leaders sort out their processes and procedures to find significant savings."

"My work tells me most people don't really know what powerful coaching is. It's not therapy or counselling—it looks forward rather than backwards. So I'm building a word-of-mouth business offering coaching experiences to help senior people work out where they are getting in their own way."

Then ask them if they know anyone like that. Someone like the person you describe. They might even say *they* have a need.

ASKING FOR ADVICE

You might want to ask your connection for advice, to pick their brains, or to see what they think of your idea.

If you're going to do that, then be aware that some people are just out to people-please, others will point to flaws in your plan, and others will help you see both sides and maybe give you suggestions. They might ask you more questions.

But the point is, there are people out there that you can talk to.

And what if you don't have a big old black book? Well, you only need a couple of people to start with. And if your network is small, the "Who do you know that I could talk to about this?" question becomes even more important.

Plants flourish when you pot them on. That is, put them in a bigger pot with fresh compost, water, light, and all that, and they will likely grow. You need to find your new pot—and that might mean getting the names and numbers of people you don't currently know. People who might be your second-degree connections.

Someone gives you a name? Awesome.

Ask: "Who else do you know?" Note—this is completely different to: "Is there anyone else you know?" Why? Because the first is an open question. The latter is closed—it can be resolved in a yes/no answer.

And that means, because we're invariably lazy, the answer will be "No".

But asking "Who do you know?" makes them think of actual people, as opposed to "No, I don't know anyone".

SUMMARY AND ACTION POINTS:

- Use LinkedIn to network and look up former colleagues. Arrange a catch up with them.
- Ask questions and be genuinely curious.
- Ask for advice, guidance, or other input.
- Ask for referrals.

ASK QUESTIONS.
BE CURIOUS
FOR THE SAKE
OF CURIOSITY.

ıeeded to do.
ıis colleagues
paying client.

a walk. Or a

perience, the

all the time.
relationship,

n you aren't
ness because
Being inter-

ing out that
they know—

on your own
nployer. You
tently doing

ow you put

n calls in a
.

ısed word—
ing to hide

AY:
CK.

ɔle. And you must come at it from the right
; to do with winning business.

. But at one time, he wasn't. He was a bloke
xchanged details, connected on LinkedIn,
distance friendship. Had a catch up every
bunch of his friends and former colleagues.

services without having even used them
d me if I could help him with his own CV.

I didn't get the job. But again, we stayed in
ɔen. I don't mean every week or even every
d catch up calls now and again. It was Dot
ınted to go it alone, as I'd seen she'd done

ıd she's referred me to many potential clients

s' group. We got on really well and became
r with what I do for a living, and so, when he
sked me to look at it with him.

We had a pizza and a beer, and I took him through what he Made a few changes myself. I did it as a favour. And when one of needed support, Ian gave the guy my details. That guy became a

You might meet a friend of a friend in the pub. At a party. Or stranger at a training course, conference, or networking event

These are the relationships that need nurturing. And in my ex best way to do that is just be your authentic, generous self.

Not by selling. That doesn't mean you have to do work for fre But by giving people an experience of who you are and building you just never know if it might turn into work in the future.

The point I'm making is that the three scenarios I've just giv examples of when I've gone out to build a network and win bus of it. This isn't a hustle. It's about genuine relationship buildin ested in people, and showing it.

I've just gone out and been me. And if those people end up fin I'm not a complete knob and that I could help them or someone well that's great, isn't it?

The 'being me' bit is important too. The advantage of going out is that you're no longer shackled to the corporate image of your e can create the reputation you want by being yourself and consi the things you want to be known for.

The things you say, the way you relate to customers' problems, yourself across, what you wear—this is all unashamedly YOU.

Amongst other things, people know me for rocking up to Zo Guns n' Roses t-shirt, and probably with a bit of fruity languag

These things are part of me just being me. I am being that ove authentic. I am most comfortable when I'm being myself, not ha a bit of me behind a corporate logo or banner.

So when you're chatting to someone who could have the potential to either become a customer, or refer one to you (someone you could serve in some way to make their lives better, regardless of whether they pay you for it), you don't have to put on the corporate façade.

It's just you, building your reputation.

The funny thing about that realisation, is that not everyone will like the real you. You need to become comfortable with that fact.

There's an argument for being polarising. If you have a style or approach that some people absolutely adore, and others hate, the chances of converting the people who love you will be much stronger than if you try to appeal to everyone. You'll become more Marmite and less, er, magnolia.

You'll find the random people you meet that get you, will get you quickly, and they are more likely to talk to other people they know who share their outlook about you.

Word of mouth, you see. Of course, you need to couple all this with great work, but great work alone will not carry you all the way.

And I've not even mentioned brand. Oh, I just did. Your brand is what other people say or think about you when you're out of the room. It's not your logo. The only way you can affect your brand is by deciding what sort of customer you want—and talking directly to them.

Will I put some people off with my potty-mouthed LinkedIn posts and blogs (and this book)? Probably. And that's fine with me, as I know the people who I want to work with are less bothered about that than what I can do to help them.

And they probably have potty mouths themselves, or secretly wish they could use them at work more often.

SUMMARY AND ACTION POINTS:

- Avoid being a dick for most of your career and the people you've worked with will remember you fondly. It compounds.
- Go out to serve people powerfully and try not to think about fees.
- Be yourself, you'll find your crowd.
- Keep in touch with people.
- Don't be a dick.

BE YOUR AUTHENTIC, GENEROUS SELF. YOU'LL FIND YOUR CROWD.

PART 3

HOW TO DO IT.

OK.

Now we've looked at what's holding you back, we can dive into how to make going it alone a reality.

In this final part, I'll take you through some of the different modes or ways of working you could adopt when going it alone.

You don't have to be an expert in any of them—I knew nothing before I started my own adventure. But this should be enough to get the juices flowing and inspire some action.

These modes are not mutually exclusive, so your business model (if you were to ever think about it in those terms) could include a mixture of them. It might sound counterintuitive, but sometimes just making it up according to what a potential client might need, simply works.

I've mentioned all of these ways of working earlier in the book, but now we're going to go into more detail. In the following chapters I will take you through becoming a service provider, day-rate contracting and interim work, passive income products (create once, sell many times), and a blended approach to going it alone.

But first, let's get a few important considerations out of the way.

CHAPTER 13
SOME WATCH-OUTS.

If you're going from full-time employment to full-time (or even part-time) self-employment, there are several home comforts that you're used to that will become history. They include:

- sick pay,
- holiday pay,
- company car,
- the same salary,
- company pension contributions,
- funded private healthcare/insurance.

But...the good news is that all these things are still available whilst working for yourself—if you want them. Most can become tax-deductible costs to your business. You just have to generate the revenue to cover them. You can buy personal health insurance online, you can lease a car, and contribute to a pension. In fact, putting into a pension is a great way of reducing your corporation tax liability. If the business is paying you a salary (and dividends) as a director, the business doesn't know whether you're working or not, or sick or not.

You will also become a one-man—(person?)—band. That is, playing all the instruments yourself. As well as doing the actual work, you become managing director, marketing director, sales director, *and* finance director. That said, I suggest searching out recommendations for an accountant to oversee your finances, especially for advising on the elements I mentioned in the last paragraph. (Don't take my word for it on this one—they will advise accordingly.)

Doing all the jobs comes with its own challenges. You are everything in the business. You create the work, deliver the work, invoice for the work... there's a lot involved. Therefore sometimes it can be hard to separate working *in* the business from working *on* the business.

Working in the business is doing the work—the delivery. Working on the business is doing the marketing, the planning, the growth activity, all the other stuff that isn't delivery. You have to get the balance right. Too much delivery and client-generating business development might suffer. Too much business development, marketing, or fannying about with a logo design, and you can quickly get behind on delivery.

It's worth thinking about what you can simplify or outsource. If you get so outrageously busy that you can't cope, consider finding a trustworthy Virtual Assistant (or 'VA') to support you with the less value-adding tasks, a designer for your logo, or just someone to help you optimise your time. As I've said already, definitely find an accountant.

You could also be on your own much of the time. No coffee counter or water cooler chats. No one to bounce things off. So sometimes it can be lonely. This is why I spend a fair amount of time on LinkedIn, as I get social 'business' interaction there as well as using it for marketing purposes. I've also built solid relationships with other freelancers and contractors both in my immediate niche and adjacent to it. I call these people my 'team'. They're my people, and they're in a similar boat to me, so we can chew ideas over together or have a whinge over a virtual coffee chat, or if we're lucky, in person.

So yes, working for yourself is great, but I'm sat here at a quarter-to-ten in the evening writing this bit as the book needs to be with the editor in two days' time. It's not going to write itself.

And there's another challenge. Going it alone can be an incredible opportunity to take back control of your life—if you get it right. I work a four-day week most weeks and have the choice to take a break here or there to cut the grass, go for a walk, play the guitar, go to one of my kids' school performances, have a sleep, or meet someone for breakfast. But in that moment I'm choosing to say "yes" to that, and "no" to work. You'll have that choice too—but be wary that the buck of income generation very clearly stops with you.

My observation from having done this for four years is that you get out of working for yourself what you put in—so long as what you put in is valuable. I was just talking to a friend who works for a company where the office folk still have to clock in and out. It's archaic presenteeism at its worst. What the employees are getting paid for is being in the office for 41 hours, not for the output they create versus their objectives. So if you're going to spend time (valuable time) on this venture, focus on the important stuff. I reckon that 20 per cent of what you do will generate 80 per cent of your income, so get that bit right and you'll be well away.

Talking of income, and building on what I told you earlier in Chapter 7 about creating a cash buffer, here's a short story:

During one of my contracts, I had the pleasure of speaking to a guy who was a career interim. I asked him for the single most important lesson he could teach me. "Build a war chest" he said.

"Make sure you cream off a percentage of your billings and put it somewhere where you either can't touch it, or it's at least separated from your other money. Do this for every paid invoice. Then it's there if you need it if, and when, you're suddenly out of contract for three months. Or six. Or more."

So contribute to your 'war chest', then you can unlock it when, you need to. Even if you've been fortunate and landed a lucrative contract straight out of your regular job's notice period, you need to start building that cash buffer. Straight away.

If you haven't been used to putting something away each month, start. Set up a standing order, or create a 'pot' in your business bank account for this. Many of the modern app-based banking systems allow you to do that either manually or through automation. No excuses. You'll thank yourself for it.

Saving a chunk of each invoice to accrue for taxes (say 25 per cent) and build your rainy-day-can't-get-another-gig pot (say 10 per cent) is more important than I can possibly emphasise.

And here's something else.

That cash is to cover your income in the event that you don't have any. Not to pay for frivolous holidays or other niceties. Skim income into another pot for that. Learn from the mistake (a 'decision'?) I made:

I was sitting pretty, business was going very well, and I'd recently registered it for VAT (meaning that I'd breached the 12-month rolling income threshold of £85,000 and begun adding tax to my invoices—whilst paying the government for the pleasure).

I'd built up a bit of a war chest, and it began burning an e-mountain bike shaped hole in my pocket. Particularly as the business could buy it and loan it to me as part of a reduced version of the Cycle to Work scheme. And it would be corporation tax deductible, AND I could claim the VAT back on it too. All too tempting. Now, I don't regret buying the bike for one moment, as it's awesome. But it was a lot of money.

Money that really should have gone to the rainy-day-war-chest-pot-fund thing, to cover me if I had a few slow weeks.

Roll on a few months and what happened? The inevitable slow weeks. It caused me to need to move money around, look at and adjust my investments, and at the same time, it created a real sense of unease, waking up the slumbering "Am I good enough?" thinking. It wasn't helpful. Don't get me wrong, we'd be alright, but if we didn't have these other fallbacks in place, it could've been a different story.

Why am I telling you all this? I don't want to put you off, but I want to make sure you understand that I've not written this book to suggest working for yourself is a bed of roses. Because it's not. It can be tough—but would you rather it be tough and be more in control of what's happening, or it be tough because work isn't stretching enough for you and your boss is a dickhead?

SAVE A CHUNK OF YOUR INVOICES FOR TAXES AND BUILD YOUR WAR CHEST.

CHAPTER 14
BECOME A SERVICE PROVIDER.

What's a service provider?

For me, the definition is along the lines of: "Providing knowledge and skill-based services with little or no inventory (stock), for money." In other words, selling what you know.

You can do this in a variety of ways. One-to-one support to individuals, or one-to-many support to groups. In person or online. Or all of these things. A mixture. There are no rules here.

You could create guides, information, courses, or templates, all in the name of service. Servicing, as discussed in Chapter 9, other people's problems.

If you consider that your ideal customer is someone a few steps behind you who wants to know how you got there, then that should get you thinking. Then consider how they would like to receive that guidance—and what encouragement they might need to buy it from you.

How did I become a service provider? Well, I didn't exactly have a plan, but with the power of hindsight I can break it down into these eight steps to create and market services aimed at consumers:

1. **I set up a service page on PeoplePerHour.com.** It's a freelancers' marketplace website where you can offer your services for a fee. The site takes a commission for helping you find the work. Once I'd written

my profile (easy) I created a couple of service options. "Experienced Recruiter will write your CV so you get shortlisted" or something similar. I put a price on it.

The jobs I landed at the start got things moving for me, and it was all financially safe as the site holds prepaid client funds in an escrow account[8]—these were released once I'd completed the job and it was signed off.

2. **I sold CV makeovers for £45.** I'd researched the other providers and in my mindset of scarcity (rather than abundance) I couldn't believe the range of prices for CV writing! It went from £30 to £500! Who the hell would pay £500 for a CV? I didn't anticipate that within two years my clients would be doing just that. But I started at just 45 quid.

3. **I publicised the service on LinkedIn and won 10 clients in the first month.** I mean, it was a steal now I think about it, but it was invaluable experience and gave me some reviews very quickly. They were crucial for social validation, demonstrating to people that I was providing a good service.

4. **I offered up some no-charge sessions to people struggling financially or who had been laid off (during the pandemic).** More kudos, LinkedIn mentions and recommendations followed.

5. **I received reviews that I could screen-grab and use on LinkedIn to further promote my business.** Usefully they were all five-star reviews, and because I became quite prolific I also rose up the leaderboard of writers on the PeoplePerHour platform. So I screen-grabbed that too. More work followed.

---

8 An escrow is a contractual arrangement in which a third party receives and disburses money or property for the primary transacting parties, with the disbursement dependent on conditions agreed to by the transacting parties. (Wikipedia)

6. **I raised my prices a little.** And a little more, and more still, until I was soon charging £150. I went from £450 monthly income to three times that in a couple of months.

7. **I became more confident posting content on LinkedIn—not purely advertising my services, or my prices, or screen-grabs of feedback, but demonstrating *authority*.** Hints, tips, and straightforward guidance (in social media world, 'value posts'), giving away free advice. I shared the demonstrable benefits people had gained from working with me too—the 'before and after' if you like.

   This helped me continue to build credibility and trust, as people could see I knew what I was talking about. As confidence built further, I started doing 'lives' on LinkedIn, like mini TV broadcasts, talking through and demonstrating how to troubleshoot CVs that weren't delivering interviews.

8. **Work volumes increased to the point where (in conjunction with my wife's salary) I was easily earning enough to cover most of my family expenses.** My reliance on savings reduced to zero after about six months.

I know many others who have done similar things, selling the knowledge they've accumulated, while still in full-time employment. It can be an incredible way to start generating an extra income, and you don't need to ditch your job to be able to do it. It is time consuming though, so be aware of that. You do actually have to put some dedicated effort in and carve out specific evenings for the work to happen in order to make an income.

Roll forward a couple of years and I can now look back at all I've learned from just doing *something*. I made up how I was going to approach it. I understood my ideal customers' problems and found ways to help them solve them—learning more and more about those problems and the solutions as I went.

That's the great thing about doing this: you never stop learning from your customers.

I'm constantly working on new ideas for ways I can serve my customers—whether it's new guides or templates (see Chapter 16 on passive income products), subscription schemes, group coaching sessions, guest lecturing in schools and universities—or all manner of other things.

Each time I'm developing new tools, methods, and services—you could say I'm making it up. And you'd be right—I'm making it up based on a quarter of a decade of experience. And you can do the same. Every new thing that anyone ever launched as a business idea was made up. Created in their heads, on a sheet of paper, or anything that could be written on.

BUSINESS TO BUSINESS ADVISORY

Actually, this section could apply to business to consumer sales too (that's how I use it), but often my clients are more likely to be looking to provide services to businesses.

One of the tools I picked up from Rich Litvin and Steve Chandler in *The Prosperous Coach* is the idea of 'creating' clients through renewed relationships with former colleagues, associates, or clients, and forging new connections with people you've become aware of through your work.

In a coaching session I had today, I helped my client visualise his ideal world in three years' time. In the present tense, I asked him to describe where in the world he was, how he was earning money and what he was getting out of life—remember the task in Chapter 5?

In the present tense, he explained he was working with startups, both as a non-executive advisor on the board, and for others as a consultant. I helped him peel the layers of the onion to describe the kinds of businesses in more detail, their size, the sectors they operated in, and the type of help he was giving them.

Remember, this is all a visualisation of what he's doing in the three years.

I then asked him how he'd found out about those contracts and had made those connections. He very quickly started joining the dots, realising that at some point he'd have needed to start creating relationships with startups and their directors. He could do that by following and them on LinkedIn and engaging in their content, attending trade shows and events, engaging with trade bodies that represent those industries, finding opportunities to deliver lectures or speeches, and so on. Not all at once, of course. "It's all about the relationships", he said.

He realised he could get on with making those new connections and start demonstrating is capability and authority in his area of expertise.

He recognised he also needed to reignite his extensive network from the middle and later parts of his career, by simply messaging or calling people for a catch up. Finding out what they are up to. Telling them what he's doing now and just having a conversation. It had to start somewhere.

Then, we discussed the idea of asking those new connections about the biggest challenges they were facing, and whether they'd be open to another conversation to see if he could shed any light on potential solutions for them—pro bono. And that conversation is where the magic of client creation happens. If you can give them a powerful experience that helps them solve a problem, or opens their eyes to new solutions, then you've proved yourself of value to them and demonstrated your authority at the same time.

The final part is to ask them if they'd like to find out what holding more of these conversations would look like—and if they say yes, they're inviting you to make a proposal to them. I offer an example in Chapter 17.

I'm really simplifying the process here that Rich and Steve wrote a whole book on (an expensive book, but one that can easily help you make a lot of money). And yes, it's aimed at people who want to up their game as professional coaches, but it's primarily about the business of coaching and creating clients, not about coaching itself. I thoroughly recommend it as I believe the principles they share would give you a new set of brilliant tools to help you grow a word-of-mouth, service-based business.

PROS

- It's enormously rewarding to sell your knowledge and to help someone solve a problem quickly.
- There's lots of variety in the work, so you will soon hear about and solve lots of problems. You can use those solutions elsewhere.
- You'll learn quickly—what's working and not working, how to give better guidance/advice, how to package what you're selling or doing.
- You'll learn from your clients and the breadth of challenges you face.
- There's a huge volume of creators on LinkedIn now that have built successful businesses online. They offer tonnes of free content (almost too much) to help you market yourself.
- You can do this outside of work hours.

CONS

- It's not easy.
- It's time consuming. Everything you do for the first time is.
- Even once you've started making money you can't predict when you'll be earning enough to cover your monthly costs.
- At some point you're likely to question why you're doing it, going to all this effort.

SUMMARY AND ACTION POINTS:

- Sell what you know, what you love, what there's a market for, and what people will pay for.
- Brainstorm these things and create your own Ikigai (have another read through Chapter 9).

- What skills and credibility do you already have that could help other people or businesses quickly, say, in an hour-long online meeting?
- Consider one simple way you can help solve a problem for a customer. Be creative, there are no rules and no wrong answers. Try that one thing for 90 days and see what happens.
- You can always change your approach later. Nothing has to be set in stone.[9]

9 While helping me edit this book, my brother directed me to the idea of GESET or 'good enough for now, safe enough to try'. It's a Sociocratic decision making and governance concept—look it up and have a read.

CHAPTER 15

GO CONTRACTING. BECOME AN INTERIM.

When we think of contracting, we might think of people that have been in or alongside our teams, sitting on the periphery, who have then come and gone without us really knowing what they were there to do.

Contracting can be a bit like that, but it really does depend on the engagement. And different contractors will have different arrangements with their clients, including where they're based and how much they should be in the office, what they're supposed to be delivering, who they need to work with—all sorts of factors. And those contracts could have been agreed in one of a variety of ways—not all contracts are equal. If you're already researching contracting as a way of working, I'll help you draw some distinctions as you may already be getting confused by some of the terminology.

TRADITIONAL 'INTERIM' CONTRACTS

Typically, interim contracts are made between your company and the client's company, and that's how most interims prefer to work. Reasons for this include the potential tax efficiencies, and the flexibility to work with different clients and on different projects.

Interim contracting means operating as a 'contractor': someone who works usually through a limited company or via an 'umbrella company' on specific projects for their client. An umbrella company is one provided by a recruitment agent that allows you to sell your services through them without needing a limited company or contracting directly with the client.[10]

And, instead of receiving a salary, your business or the agent charges the client an hourly (or more likely a daily) rate, usually billed monthly. As a contractor you then take a salary from your own business, along with dividends as means of payment. It's a business-to-business relationship with the client, not an employee-employer relationship. You will find some contracts are described as 'interim assignments'.

Interim contracts can be either full or part-time, and usually become available because a company or organisation has a specific piece of work, project, or programme they need completing that requires a set of skills not available internally (and which might otherwise be delivered through a secondment or as extra responsibility), and that has a particular timescale. Often, they want someone with a completely new approach, viewpoint, or 'pair of eyes' to assess what's required and then deliver it.

In my experience, companies that require contractors have a specific need or problem they want solving. That could be to scope and/or deliver a particular project, troubleshoot some area of the business, or to bring specific industry knowledge or expertise into a team for a period of time. And that could be anything from a few weeks to two years.[11]

You may find yourself talking to clients about part-time contracts where they need you a day a week or so many days a month dedicated to delivering their work. One of my clients has recently agreed to such a contract, working five days a month for their client at their premises, helping them sort out a range

---

10 Agencies and clients often have these agreements in place when the client has a laborious service provider onboarding process, simplifying the contracting process for you and for them. You'd get paid by the agency, and normally you'd need to submit approved timesheets.

11 Any longer than two years and you might get in hot water with HMRC. If it's more than two years, you start to gain employment rights, and the HMRC might consider your work as less of a short-term requirement and more a substantive role. Watch out.

of HR challenges. You should gauge and discuss the requirements through those initial conversations, and agree (and contract) timescales, deliverables, amount of dedicated time, locations, and pay rates before any work starts. More on that in a bit.

IR35—'OFF-PAYROLL' WORKING

IR35 legislation was introduced in the UK in 2000 with the aim of preventing disguised employment, closing the loophole of companies engaging contractors ('off-payroll') in a way that closely resembles employment rather than via a genuine business-to-business relationship. Doing so would have enabled them to avoid paying sick pay, National Insurance Contributions (NICs), and benefits, and removed notice periods, while the contractor enjoyed a level of tax efficiency too. You can see why the government might have wanted to address this.

When introduced, it was the contractor's responsibility to determine whether a contract was deemed 'inside' or 'outside' IR35, however the government long believed that contractors had been abusing the rules and so introduced IR35 reform—so it's now nearly always up to the client to assess the IR35 status of the contract.

In short, if the contract is deemed 'outside IR35', you will be able to show you are truly self-employed, and that you pay yourself through your limited company (sometimes referred to as a personal service company or PSC).

If it's 'inside IR35', HMRC views this as an employment relationship and you'll pay Income Tax and NICs, just like an employee.

There are several distinctions ('tests') that your client should use to determine the IR35 status that have been tested in case law.

Those distinctions include to what degree you are supervised or directed in the role (i.e., you have a 'boss' rather than a 'client'?), and how much control the client has over what you do and how you do it. Further, is there a 'mutuality of obligation'—that is, is your client obliged to offer you work beyond the agreed project and are you obliged to accept it? Other considerations include whether you use your own equipment (like laptops and phones), if you are seen as 'one of the team', and whether (in the instance where you make a mistake), you fix it on billed time or your own time.

The rules might have changed since releasing this book, and even if they haven't, I urge you to do your own research on it. There are many contractors' forums online, plus of course the **gov.uk** website that will give you the latest information.

FIXED TERM CONTRACTS

Some contracts are advertised as Fixed Term Contracts, or FTCs. FTCs are essentially the same as an employment contract, with all the regular benefits (and monthly salary) but with a fixed end date—say in six, eight or 12 months' time, depending on what's required. You won't work via your business, you're an employee. That means you'll be salaried, pay tax and NICs (as will the client/employer), accrue holiday, and be eligible for sick pay. FTCs also carry a notice period and offer less flexibility to work for other companies.

I embarked on a full-time FTC before I officially went self-employed. Funnily enough the initial six-month FTC was extended by another six months, and then my position was made permanent, and I stayed a further three years. It was that role that I left to go contracting 'proper'.

HOW DO I GET CONTRACTS?

Contract opportunities usually appear on the all-market online job boards like **TotalJobs.com** and **Indeed.com** but will also appear on the regular sector-specific equivalents. Research is important. Carry out searches and filter for 'job type', selecting 'contract' and/or 'temporary'. See what comes up for your specialism.

In my experience, applying for a contract role was largely the same as applying for a permanent role, in that I needed to send a CV to the company or the recruiter to apply. So you need to have your CV prepared and ready to go. If you do not have any contracting experience, this is OK, at least it was for me, however some clients may specifically look for prior interim experience.

Your CV and LinkedIn profile should evidence your ability to get moving quickly, build relationships fast, gather and understand requirements, and make an impact—or 'hit the road running'. I don't mean just saying the words. Add examples in the bullet points that bring these skills to life. Like having to respond quickly to a brief, having tight timescales, working to a budget, building stakeholder relationships, influencing—all these will be in the toolkit of a contractor in most professions.

I've built a business around writing CVs and helping contractors manage what become quite unwieldy documents, so if you need support with this, **feel free to get in touch via QR code** later in the book.

Talk to recruiters too. When you search for roles, you'll start to see the same recruitment firms popping up, and often even the same recruiters. Many recruitment firms have dedicated temporary contractor recruiters, so get to know them.

Remember though, it's not their job to get you a job. Their job is to fill their client's need, and you are their product. But there's nothing stopping you picking up the phone to a recruiter and having a conversation with them about the market, day rates, your experience, roles they have on the go—start feeling your way around the market. This research will help build your confidence—it certainly did for me.

It'll do no harm to acquaint yourself, but don't overdo it. Calling them and emailing them daily, or even every couple of weeks to see if they have any new roles will just piss them off and won't win you any friends. A quick update email once every four-to-six weeks may let them know you're still around and interested.

Likewise, avoid blanket applications for jobs in the same company. Recruiters will quickly become frustrated, and they'll likely see you as a 'serial applicant'. Sadly this comes with the potential to end up looking a bit desperate, and you don't want that. Better to be deliberate, intentional, and really objective about what you apply for.

GETTING HIRED

Expect the selection process to be markedly different to traditional employment interviews. It will vary from place to place, but usually, contractors will not go through the same full-on process that a potential employee will. You might be 'interviewed', but in my experience this has been more of a business conversation about the problem or challenge they have, the outcome they want to achieve, and whether or not I could deliver it.

The conversation may take place off site, as the recruitment of a contractor might be sensitive to the business for all sorts of reasons. I've had such meetings in motorway services cafés and corners of pubs, the 'Costa downstairs', as well as in the client's on-site restaurant. You might meet one or many of the stakeholders during the process. Your potential manager (in the language of an employee) is now your potential client.

Expect to be asked lots of questions about your experience, but also expect the client to provide you with much more information than you might expect to receive in any interview process for a job. And this, for me, is the biggest difference, and also the greatest opportunity for you to demonstrate your credentials as a specialist through asking awesome questions.

Remember that they're likely to be looking for someone with a different or new set of skills and experiences. Having someone turn up and ask questions to understand their ideas, plans, objectives, and how those objectives align with what the rest of the business is doing, is likely to impress them—and really make them think about what it is they're looking to achieve.

Asking great questions (based on your experience of delivering similar outcomes as an employee) will also help you demonstrate awareness of the likely challenges, issues, and risks that their project might entail or uncover.

This process goes both ways, too. Critically, asking insightful questions will help you evaluate the scope, get a sense of the personalities involved, whether the business generally uses contractors (or if this is a one-off), and decide whether it's something you really want to take on. And if you think the pay rate is pitched correctly.

Great generic questions include:

- What's the main challenge you're facing as a business right now?
- How does this project fit into/contribute to solving it?
- What will delivering this enable for the business?
- What have you already tried? What worked/didn't work? Why?
- Who else in the business has an interest in this, and what is their interest?
- What happens if this isn't delivered?
- Where are your biggest gaps skillswise right now?
- What's most likely to hinder or derail this project?
- What's the hunger or appetite for this piece of work elsewhere in the business?
- What's your team structure and how do you see this role fitting in?
- What budget do you have for the project?
- What flexibility is there on work location?
- Are there any politics or personalities I need to be aware of?
- If you could achieve one thing inside a month, what would it be?
- Where do you expect this piece of work to be in three/six months?
- What will success look like at the end of the assignment?
- What other resources are available in the business? (And who else can support me?)
- What scope is there for the contract to be extended beyond the initial term?

...and any other question that helps you scope or contextualise what's needed.

Use your own sector-specific knowledge to ask more focused questions about their challenge or objective—that's how the meeting can really become an informed discussion that enables you to showcase your skills.

Asking these sorts of questions will help you come across as someone who knows what they are doing. It'll help you build trust, and crucially will help you get clear on their requirements and expectations.

I recommend dropping in short examples of when you've handled similar situations or challenges as a kind of proof, like "when I delivered *x* project at *x* company, they wanted to achieve *x*, so my approach was *x* and that achieved *x*" too.

Try to avoid giving an entire game plan or solution in the interview. This is not a free consulting session. You might want to hint at a couple of ideas or overarching concepts you have but try to keep your detailed thoughts to yourself. Think of the project cycle as: scoping/problem statement, discovery, design, build, deploy, evaluate.

Different contracts will require different skills, such as influencing difficult stakeholders, communication, planning, risk analysis—you'll know what's relevant to your sector and role type, and by asking those great questions early on, and building as building a clear brief will ultimately enable you to explain how you can help them. Personally I think this is how normal job interviews should be held too (opening up to the candidate to ask the questions), but that's another story.

Something else worth thinking about is that it's OK for you to bring a different perspective, or challenge their thinking. I've been to several interviews over the years for permanent and contract roles where they really were looking for new ways of doing things. I've been tasked with reviewing recruitment websites and processes to give a headline assessment based on my experience.

The first time I didn't quite go as far as the company was looking for me to go—as they knew what they had was terrible and outdated and were looking for me to tear it up and suggest starting again rather than making tweaks. I still got the job though. The second time I went to town, recommending a complete overhaul, and this also contributed to me getting the job.

DAY RATES AND WHAT TO CHARGE

This will be guided by the market for your services, and how skilled or experienced you are. However, don't just be guided by your last (or current) salary divided by the number of working days in the year (generally considered to be 222). Your day rate should be *more than* your equivalent salary and package.

So, say your salary package (including pension contributions, car allowances, etc.) is £55,000, and assuming you're going for a similar role in a similar sector, you might think your day rate would be £248 (£55,000/222). I'm pleased to tell you that you can charge more than that.

Why?

When a business takes on the services of a contractor they're bringing in someone with a special set of skills that the business needs—but only for a relatively short time. And when you're salaried, the business also pays employers' National Insurance Contributions, and for all the benefits you'd normally receive. So comparing a contract with a permanent role is like comparing apples with potatoes.

Also, you'll want to charge more than £248 to:

- provide cover for your own financial risks (times you aren't billing and earning, like holidays, sickness absence, other types of leave);
- balance the fact that you are much more dispensable than a salaried employee and have little or no notice;
- recognise you're offering the flexibility to come and resolve a problem without all the other costs of employing a person;
- allow for the costs you'll face like paying for equipment, software licences, travel, accommodation, and so on.

So you charge £350. Or £400. Or £500.

If it helps, as a mid-level manager in 2-3,000-employee companies, earning £55-60,000, I went from charging £350 per day to £600 per day inside two years (2014 to 2016). This was partly due to the market location (I went from the Midlands to London), partly due to the fast growth and desirability of my skill set, and partly due to the client being a 'good payer' in a market known for great rates and salaries (financial services). Other interims were charging far less, and others much (much) more in the HR/project delivery world. Your skills and market will define your rate. Your earlier research around the contracts being advertised will also help you build a picture of what companies are paying for similar expertise.

FLEX YOUR NEGOTIATING MUSCLES

The main things you're likely to need to negotiate are your:

- day rate,
- location (like how frequently you need to be at the client's location, if at all),
- flexibility over delivery (say, if you do dedicated full days or two days spread over a week),
- delivery scope within the given timescale,
- holidays.

I've had negotiations with clients in the past where they have tried to align my day rate with an employee's salary. I've politely reminded them that their salaried employee will also carry on-costs (NICs, sick pay, holidays, pensions, benefits) that I won't be taking, and that they're paying a premium for the flexibility to have me come and go without being a permanent number in their headcount and payroll.

You don't want to be a knob about it, but you should stand your ground in these sorts of negotiations.

You shouldn't get pulled into the "What's your current salary?" conversation that people often experience in an employment-style interview. But you might get "What's your day rate?". If you're engaging via an external recruiter, they should already know the client's preferred rate or range for the contract—so it's out in the open. But if you're engaging directly, they may not have shared it yet.

Contractors often have a current day rate they quote in these situations, but be careful not to wildly under or overcook this. A good way to respond is: "It really varies according to the deliverables, the length of the contract, extent of travel and whether I can expense it back to you. Have you a budget in mind?"

And if they're still not forthcoming I advise providing them with a range—so have one ready. The range should be what you'll accept without feeling like you've been taken for a ride (so the 'ideal' figure), plus an aspirational percentage, say 10, 15, or 20 per cent more.

So, say I had been charging £450 a day, and wanted £500, but thought the market could withstand £600, I'd say "Well normally I'm working in the £5-600 bracket—how does that sit with you?". (This is a real-life example, and we agreed on £550. When it came to renewal, I upped it to £600.)

Like any negotiations though, you'll get better at it the more you do, and the more contracts you deliver the more you'll get to know your market rate. And when you think the client is taking the piss.

LOCATION

This should just be a sensible discussion. It's really useful to spend time at the client's office or site, especially at the start and even more so if most of your stakeholders are regularly there. However, there's not much point in you being there if the people you need to work with are elsewhere in the world or the things you're going to work on don't take place there.

I found a good mix of remote working and client site days meant that I had focused time to take care of delivery, balanced with important relationship-building face-to-face time. That was particularly important for holding big meetings, contributing to or leading workshops, or delivering presentations. This was all pre-pandemic however, but now in 2024 the 'back to the office' approach has become much more commonplace.

Like accepting a permanent job, don't end up agreeing to lengthy daily travel if your gut tells you it's not going to be sustainable for any period of time. Sure, you could get a place (a hotel, Airbnb, or a friend's spare room like I did) for a couple of nights a week, but accommodation costs will eat into your profits and erode your day rate. It's your choice, and just something to be wary of.

Therefore, you should also agree on what you're prepared to contribute to travel-wise. Some clients just expect you to turn up and do the work, regardless of where you live. When I was in the office at London Stock Exchange most days (whilst living in the Midlands and paying my own travel costs), I was fortunate to be able to regularly stay overnight at a friend's house (that was a commutable distance into London).

With another client, because I wasn't going to be spending a lot of time in the office, we agreed that I'd pay my own way to the most local office, and expense any train fares and mileage beyond that to the client at cost—as the need for me to be in any given location would be project and needs specific. You'll be able to expense these costs to your own business anyway as they are tax deductible—I recommend talking to your accountant about this.

DELIVERY

Much like location, this should be a sensible discussion. My first contract was three days a week and I agreed to work them over five days, mixing remote work with time in the office—keeping track of the time I was spending. That worked well and tied in with my second contract, which overlapped the first, as I was able to combine their two days with the other three.

But some contracts may demand five full days of your time. And those days should be contracted accordingly—whether it's seven-and-a-half or eight hours of working time. As you get into contracting, you'll probably find that some days you'll work slightly longer, and some slightly less. Again, have that discussion with your client about how you'd both prefer to play it.

You'll need a way to record your time for submitting with your invoices. If your services are being taken via an umbrella company or agency, they'll give you a timesheet (most likely online) to complete each week or month along with any expenses incurred. If you're contracting direct through your own company, then a simple spreadsheet detailing the hours and days you've been carrying out work will do the job. You can then submit that with your invoice. This is very different to the 'service provider' mode in the previous chapter, where you would normally bill either up front (as I do), or on delivery of a project or piece of work.

SCOPE

Establish the key deliverables before the contract stage. Your contract will normally be a standard 'contract for services' provided either by your company or the client, with an addendum called a schedule, covering a Statement of Works.

This will describe exactly what they want you to deliver, in what format, and by when. You need to ask the right and detailed questions to get to what is and isn't in scope to avoid confusion or assumptions being made by either party. They might fill this in, or they might ask you to. It has to be right, as you're both agreeing to it!

Whilst you might be itching to get a contract signed, it's crucial to slow down a bit and contract on the deliverables expected of you, AND what the client will provide to enable you to complete the work. You should include a change process clause in the agreement to ensure an appropriate process for altering the scope of your delivery.

This will help you avoid 'scope creep'—that is, growing numbers of deliverables. Whilst you'd think having more stuff to do would be great, they might just expect you to do that within the term of the contract. Sure, agree additional scope, but contract on what that means in terms of additional delivery time (a contract extension), or whether something else currently in scope needs to come out. In other words, make your client prioritise what they want delivered, and use that change process clause to nail it down so everyone is clear on what you're doing and what you're getting paid for.

You can also use the schedule to confirm all the other elements you agree on, then everyone knows where they are.

HOLIDAYS

If you plan to have time off (more than a couple of days) you'll want to mention this during your early discussions. Although you're a service provider, the client is unlikely to expect you to be pedal-to-the-metal for the entire duration. You're not a big consulting firm, you're you, albeit supplied by your personal service company. And you may have holiday commitments. Just be honest and open about them early in discussions and check if that's likely to present any problems. It's more than likely that members of their employed team (who may also be engaged in your project) will need to take time off during your engagement and, in my experience, clients are pretty reasonable about this.

In a world where your next contract comes straight after the previous one finishes, you're not going to get time off. But I would strongly (that is STRONGLY) recommend taking at least a week or two between contracts, however tempting it is to reach for the juicy carrot that is your day rate.

Contracting can be intense and nose-down. You must take time to rest, reset, and recuperate. Sure, you're not earning while you're on holiday, AND you're paying for the holiday, so it can feel like the holiday has cost you twice as much. It really can. And that can feel very painful. You're losing two or three grand in pay and paying four grand for a holiday, so the holiday is now £7,000. But remember, this is why you charge more than the equivalent salary as a day rate. If it helps, mentally roll the holiday time into the period of your contract, and then divide your total billings by all the days.

So £500/day x 50 days = £25,000.

Add on 10 days' holiday (so 60 days) and that same £25,000 yields £416/day.

Or, if you know about your two-week holiday in advance, and you're talking about a six-month contract, you could try to negotiate it to six months and two weeks to offset your time off and assure your income.

Either that, or just be comfortable that you bill for the days you work, and for the days you don't, you don't—but you get free time and flexibility to do other things, including rest. You must do that if you want to avoid burnout.

Importantly, most people forget while they're making a living to also make a life. Interim contracting is a lifestyle choice as much as a career choice.

Contracting (particularly if it's part-time or, say, 10 days' consulting over the course of two months) should become a lifestyle choice as well as a way of earning money.

It's entirely possible the reason you're looking at working for yourself in the first place is to get more control over your time. In which case you should take a look at your finances and lifestyle to determine what 'enough' income is, and work backwards from that to work out how many days a week/month/year you want to work. I know plenty of people who have arranged their contracts to end in July so they can take two months off over the summer and engineer the next to start in September. It's not always possible, but it's definitely more possible than it is for someone in a permanent job.

INVOICING

Invoicing is really the same however you plan to go it alone but I'll address it here. If you don't yet have an online accounting system (I didn't for the whole time I was contracting, only taking the plunge to **Quickbooks** and then **Xero** once my services shifted to largely consumer-facing), it's pretty straight forward and can be done in **Microsoft Excel**.

Excel has multiple templates for writing invoices. Just choose one, or take a look at them and create your own template that you can use again and again. I'd share the one I used but honestly the ones now available in Excel are far better. You can personalise them with a logo and invoice numbers. They're very good.

Create another spreadsheet to record your invoices and dates, clients, their email addresses, value, VAT, paid/due/overdue... your accountant will thank you and it's good practice to keep these kinds of records anyway. Just make a new entry each time you send an invoice.

Your client will probably have a monthly pay run scheduled by their finance team, and you should find out from your client contact when that is and what their standard payment terms are. You can always try to negotiate faster payment than their standard 30, 60 or heaven forbid, 90 days—but get it written into your contract for services. In my experience it's wise to go and make friends with the people in Accounts Payable so they can put a face to a name when it comes to processing your invoice. Cakes might be a nice touch too.

If you're working through an agency, this pain is taken away from you and managed by them on your behalf. In fact, they'll most likely pay you before they've even been paid by the client—because your contract is with *them*, and *their* contract is with *the client*. Effectively, you're their product, so they'll want to keep you happy.

DRY SPELLS AND RENEWALS

As a contractor I had periods when I didn't have any work. But there were times when I got referred to my next project by new connections I'd made in the previous contract, so had them virtually back-to-back. If you're on a day-rate contract (or FTC), as you head towards the closing period, it's time to start having the 'what's next?' conversation with your client. Often a contract that starts out as a three-month piece of work might have the scope to extend by a further three, six, or nine months.

In fact, it's a good idea to agree with the client at the outset a) whether or not there's scope for extension at all, and then b) when you should be having renewal conversations with them. If it's not written into the contract, establish a verbal agreement with them. I'd advise doing this at advanced negotiations/discussions rather than in the first chat. It can go like this:

"It's great that we've agreed on an initial three months. I think we've both established there's more scope in the work than three months, probably six to nine. When do you think it would be good for us to talk about potential to extend? How about week ten?"

If the answer is "Yes", and you are happy with that, you are OK to say: *"Great. Once I get started, are you happy for me to put in half an hour with you that week to discuss it?"*

This is about establishing certainty with some verbal contracting, for the benefit of both parties. If you're performing, are on track, and they like you, they're not going to want to let you go to another contract if there's more work to do. It might even give you more bargaining power.

Either way, you want to continue keeping your ear to the ground, building your network, finding out about opportunities—so if it's not renewed (or worse still the contract is foreshortened, or you decide to leave), you're hopefully able to jump onto another piece of work.

PROS

- You will likely learn much more than you've ever learned, and much more quickly than in any employed role.
- You can largely avoid politics as you're there and being paid to 'do a specific job' and get in and get out.
- You can build a strong network of managers, peers, suppliers, and other contractors to help you hear about new roles.
- It can pay VERY well compared to a salaried role.

CONS

- You're taking a risk. You may do a six-month contract, or it might be 18 months. Then you might not land on a project for months after. If you're terrible at building a network and saving money, these are skills you'd do well to learn.
- You don't receive *any* company benefits. No sick pay. You might want to contribute into your own pension. You need to make sure you pay yourself enough to qualify for state pension too (ask your accountant).
- It's challenging. You get very little running-in period before you're expected to make an impact. Building an internal network quickly, learning knowing which levers to pull—you'll need to crack on and not waste any time.
- You might get the feeling of being out of your depth. I did. But I was learning and doing new things quickly whilst trying to build relationships.
- Contracts carry small notice periods. It might be a week, or a month, or nothing at all—you can put this in your contract. So be prepared: if it's going south and looking likely to end, you need a decent network to rely on to help you into a new role. Hopefully it won't, but as the volume of jobs you take on increases, one's bound to go awry.

Contracting in the way I've described may or may not be for you. It might be perfect for you on its own, or it might be something you can offer as part of your services. It doesn't have to be all or nothing. I've done it on a full-time basis and become a career interim, and have offered odd days of paid consultancy alongside my 'service provider' private work. Make it work for you.

MY TOP TIPS

1. **Confirm your day rate and invoicing/payment schedule, scope, location, delivery approach, and any holidays, up front.** This will save you all sorts of problems and difficult conversations later, and above all it's just a professional way to manage the engagement.

2. **Establish a routine of one-to-ones with your client to update them on progress/resolve issues, and gain feedback.** Agree an agenda with the client. And find out how they would prefer to be contacted if you need some support on something outside that cadence? On that note...

3. **Know your escalation route.** Agree and document this early in the assignment, if not at contract stage. If you've tried your powers of influence and you're not getting anywhere with a stakeholder (and it's adding risk to your timelines), know to whom, where, and how to raise it. Is it a phone call? A registered risk? A coffee? An email? The same could be said for any other upcoming risk you've identified. Your client will not like surprises, so keep them informed of risks (preferably with some mitigation ideas—they're not there to just solve your problems for you). If you don't inform them they'll find out late, probably too late, and they'll be pissed, as might other senior stakeholders. Not good. Remember: they want you to succeed and they're on your side.

4. **Volunteer a 'state of the nation' report in the first week of your assignment.** That could be a SWOT analysis of the things you've seen or heard that pertain to your contract, like processes you believe are over-complicated, labour intensive, or broken (or conversely, working really well), quick-win opportunities, longer-term challenges, that sort of thing. Your client will likely appreciate the value of your fresh perspective and experience of working in other organisations. It might even provide you with levers to extend the scope or duration of your engagement. As I've said already, be careful though to not add to the scope if you're not extending the contract. You could keep additional scope up your sleeve to broach in the run up to extension.

5. **Use your client contact.** They are effectively sponsoring you into your role, and they'll have a vested interest in your success. Get to know them. Ask them about the challenges in the business, and what certain stakeholders like or dislike in the way of communication or influencing style. Find out what levers there are to help you progress quickly, and

who in the business will support you—and who might get in your way, and what they've learned from dealing with them.

6. **Get to know people in the business.** Talk with people in your wider team and stakeholders on your projects. Take them for a coffee. Find out what they do, what they're trying to achieve in their roles. Where were they before? What are their ambitions? It will also help you quickly get the scoop on upstream challenges in your project, or insights on personalities, and nuances that you just won't get in the interview stages.

   As your assignment continues, carry on networking around the business. You may hear of other potential work opportunities you can assist with in the weeks after your contract ends. I am still talking to many of the people I connected with in my contracts eight years later. Some many have become my clients—either in day-rate corporate work or personally. I have had thousands of pounds worth of one-to-one work come through people who were stakeholders or on the fringes of my contract work.

7. **Be helpful and reasonable.** Just don't be a dick. Deliver on your contracts, and the people you meet will help you grow your network. I can't over-emphasise this point. Build good relationships both with your employed colleagues and other contractors.

CONTRACTING MIGHT BE FOR YOU IF:

- You like variety.
- You don't mind a bit of risk.
- You like getting stuck into a project.
- You have three months' savings, preferably more.
- You're able to build relationships and trust quickly.
- You are happy to carve your way through ambiguity.
- You're open to travel, and perhaps getting digs elsewhere during the week.

CONTRACTING IS LESS LIKELY FOR YOU IF:

- You dislike uncertainty.
- You're a creature of habit.
- You aren't great at forging relationships quickly.
- You're a homebird—unless you live in a city with lots of opportunities so you don't need to travel far.

SUMMARY AND ACTION POINTS:

- Build a CV that showcases your skills and experience, and positions you as a contractor.
- Search job boards for contract roles (preferably outside IR35—for latest guidance search "IR35 rules"). What skills do they need and what are they paying?
- Speak to the recruiters advertising their roles. Find out how quickly those companies need to hire. Ask if your CV positions you well as a contractor? Get a feel for the market, roles, projects, and day rates.
- Save three-to-six months' money or have someone like a family member who can back you for a short while if needed.
- Agree and document terms and the scope of your work, and what to do when something outside of scope comes along.
- When you're in a contract, network like crazy. Your future business will depend on it.

ASK INSIGHTFUL QUESTIONS AND YOU'LL SHOWCASE YOUR EXPERTISE MORE THAN IN ANY GREAT ANSWER.

CHAPTER 16

SELL PASSIVE INCOME PRODUCTS.

In 2022, a good two years into trading, I started having a think about passive products—but you can do this straight away. In fact, it's a great way of getting going, though it helps if you've started to build authority in the market, most likely through LinkedIn.

What's a passive income product? It's a 'create once, sell many' concept. Examples include:

- Lists
- Forms
- Templates
- Swipe files
- Process maps
- How-to guides
- Any other asset you've either already created or might easily put together that someone else would find useful.

More complex products could include eBooks, online training courses and videos, all of which could act as low or no-cost lead magnets for your consulting offers.

I did this with an annotated CV template marked up with notes, guidance, and example wording. I recorded a simple video to go with it. It's not flashy or slick. I sold it on **Gumroad.com**.

I progressed and started recording short videos and uploading them to YouTube and began sharing them with a few clients who turned down the offer of working with me one-to-one. I gave them free access to these tools on the basis that they gave me feedback so I could improve them.

Once I was happy enough with them (and they are by no means polished) I locked down the YouTube links and bundled them with the CV template to sell. There are many online ecommerce sites to choose from to enable you to do this—some charge a monthly fixed fee but no commission (like **Samcart**) and some the other way round (like **Gumroad**) that don't charge a monthly fee but do take a 10 per cent commission.

Each allows some level of customisation, but you get a simple homepage you can direct people to that advertises your stuff.

Before you begin spending huge amounts of time developing these assets, it's worth pre-selling them first. This is the process of going out to the market to see if anyone really wants to buy them.

There are several ways of doing this, including:

- LinkedIn posts—issuing polls to learn the most valuable tools people might buy;
- text-based posts that offer value—when traction grows and a post gains more views and comments, you know it's a hot topic;
- online waiting lists—you can build these into your website if you choose to have one, or find a standalone waitlist management app (like **ConvertKit.com**) that you can direct people to and collect their email addresses. You can then use that database to mail out special offers on your products, offer more value, or simply notify them that the product is coming. I did this very thing in pre-selling this book.

Whichever you use you'll have to collect data on whether the thing you want to create will be valuable to people (and will be in demand). If it's not, you can tweak it and experiment again, or move on quickly to another idea.

Personally, I don't make a huge income through my passive products (which also include original greetings card designs sold on **Thortful.com**), but I know some people who are much better at it than me (that is, they've spent a lot of time honing their audience, their message, promoting their products) and make a monthly four- (or even five-) figure sum from their digital products all on their own. I consider these products as low-cost, low-risk ways to drive awareness of me and my services, and to have an experience of working with me. And over time, customers might move towards my higher ticket offers. So I don't expect to make a fortune directly from them in their own right.

It is definitely worth doing, particularly if you can create something quickly that people will find extremely useful. Just keep marketing it, at least once a week in your LinkedIn posts.

SUMMARY AND ACTION POINTS:

- Create quickly and test.
- Don't over-think your products.
- Pre-sell your products.
- Keep up with the marketing, and feature the products in your LinkedIn Featured section.

CHAPTER 17

THE BLENDED APPROACH.

Put simply, the blended approach is a combination of passive sales, ad hoc consulting or service provision, and interim work. Having flexibility over what you do and when will pay dividends if/when things get quiet.

In fact, the quiet times are an ideal opportunity to dedicate some time to creating a passive product or producing value content on LinkedIn.

HOWEVER! Be wary.

Don't try to do everything at once.

I'd love to say have a strategy, and that would be great advice, but I would say...

JUST START.

That's it.

Because like I've said already, the timing will never be right.

You'll never be 'ready'.

So if you think a blended approach might be for you, or you just don't know the right route yet, simply do *something*.

Particularly if you've not got that much time but you're desperate to jack in the nine-to-five and tell them where to stick it.

But if you're going to start, pick one thing and start with that.

When I was starting my second attempt to go-it-alone, my 'start with one thing' was a simple CV re-writing service. I found **PeoplePerHour.com** and set up a profile, and launched a CV writing service, at £45 a time.

This generated 10 clients inside a month, but more than that it generated lots of interest in just a week.

My mind started racing. "What else can I do?!" I thought to myself. "Ah yes! I can write job descriptions. I've done loads of those, to a high standard, and job descriptions are usually terrible. I'll offer that!"

So I created a new product on PeoplePerHour and advertised it on LinkedIn aaaaaand..... nothing. Nada. Zip. Sweet Jack Shit.

My former boss Lisa, who is also a great coach, said to me: "Phil, you're trying to do too many things at once. Besides the fact that selling B2B is a completely different ballgame to B2C...just choose one thing and do it for 90 days.

"Iterate it along the way, sure. Put your prices up. But focus on doing it, get really, really good at it, and become known for that thing."

And I did. And this was the best piece of advice I could have possibly received at that crucial time.

It was only after that period that I added any new products or services. The next one was interview coaching.

And combined, those two offerings remained my bread and butter for two-and-a-half years before I started building out my coaching practice.

But they didn't stay exactly the same. I learned quickly, continued to ask for feedback, and figured out that I could offer different packages, such as a 'Silver' CV review and feedback, a 'Gold' full consultation and rewrite, and a 'Platinum' service with other bells and whistles.

Former colleague and friend Quentin said: "Consider packages. People like a little choice." Once, a client had told me in no uncertain terms I was offering incredible value. I asked him what he might have paid (instead of the £150 he actually paid). £250 was the answer, but he added he'd want some kind of one-to-one for that. Previously I'd just rewritten the CV based on what was already there and a couple of examples of target job specs.

He went on to promote my services wildly around his business—which was going through a massive redundancy programme—and I picked up thousands of pounds' worth of clients from his referrals.

At the same time this was going on, a former colleague from one of my earlier interim roles (she happened to be the HR Director) approached me out of the blue, having seen my posts on LinkedIn telling my followers that I was working for myself again.

She said she had a project to review their recruitment processes and give some recommendations, and would I be interested? Well, of course I was. We met up in a salubrious but mutually accessible location (a motorway services café) and we talked about the challenge she was facing.

I listened to what she had to say, asked lots of questions about what she wanted to achieve, answered her questions whilst demonstrating authority and capability, took lots of notes and started to form a loose brief.

At the end we agreed there was mutual interest and I asked her what she thought the best next steps would be, which were for us to have a follow up call to get into more detail.

From there I created a draft proposal to ensure I'd captured the brief, the deliverables, and the timelines. Once that was agreed I proposed a rate, and we entered a negotiation that resulted in me being awarded the project.

I secured 10 days of consulting work, to be carried out remotely, which I was able to do between my other private one-to-one work, blog writing, passive product creating, and everything else. And those 10 days led to a further 10 days over the next couple of months with new but related deliverables.

That engagement came to me by virtue of the work I'd done before, the promotion I'd been doing on LinkedIn, and effectively my reputation, mixed with a bit of 'not being a dick'. I hope. What I'm saying here is that any of the ideas and strategies in this book can be blended together to help you find work and help work find you.

The thing about receiving inbound work is that you never know when it's going to come along. But you can adapt any of the tools I've described already to approach former connections and colleagues for a catch up. You can bring them up to date with what you're doing, like I described in Chapter 14. You never know what will come from that conversation.

SUMMARY AND ACTION POINTS:

- Avoid getting bogged down in creating a strategy. Sometimes just doing something will help you get a feel for whether it's the right or wrong thing.
- Experiment. Your business, your rules.
- Don't expect overnight success. It may take months of full-time graft to start turning over a basic income.
- Find ways of packaging or bundling up elements of your service to drive higher value sales.
- Do a great job and your customers will do your marketing for you.

TRY DOING SOMETHING FOR 90 DAYS, THEN TWEAK.

CONCLUSION.

CHAPTER 18

WHAT'S NEXT?

We're closing in on the end of the book, dear soloist-in-waiting.

In a moment I'm going to tell you a couple of stories to bring this read to a close, but before that, a recap.

Here's what we've covered together:

1. **In the first few chapters of the book, we dived into the self-limiting stories we tell ourselves.**

   The stories that stop us from making a start with something we really want to do. You explored the reasons you're giving yourself and the excuses you're making for not getting started.

   We looked at dispelling thoughts of not being good enough. We built a case to show you that you're better than you think you are, and certainly have knowledge and capability that puts you ahead of the people that would pay you for it.

   You don't need to be an out-and-out expert with degrees and plaudits and an all-time record in your specialised subject on Mastermind; you just need to be a few steps ahead of the people that need help.

2. **You reflected on the things you'd need in order to get going, and we had a good look at bravery and how to get better at developing it without have to go full bore and commit.**

   We visualised what the brave new world could look like. You gained permission to think big and think small at the same time. You should now have a clear picture of what possibilities lay ahead of you, along with an idea of the mindset and skills you might need.

3. **We established that no time is the right time so you might as well just start now.**

   There are multitudes of people who have taken big steps at all points in their lives. It's never too late. Or too soon.

   And crucially, that 'readiness' is in your mind. We're never 100 per cent ready for anything. There's always something to upset the applecart and throw a spanner in the works. And in fact, getting a service or product out can be a great experiment: it might not cover everything you want it to cover, but does your target customer want everything you can offer in one go?

   Probably not. Remember, be of service to people a few steps behind you, or even coming from ground zero—they might just need the basics of what you can offer.

   By the end of this section, you'd realised that getting to 80 or even 60 per cent 'ready' and just going for it will not only get you off the mark but also help you learn extremely quickly.

4. **We looked at your finances.**

   Money (and lifestyle) is always a massive contributing factor in big life decisions, and sometimes the driver for them too. We established that having six months of savings isn't necessary to put yourself out in the world and sell what you know. You don't even have to quit your job.

You should now have a better understanding than ever of what's been holding you back and how relatively straightforward it is to get going.

However, I also challenged you to take a sensible look at your spending habits and create a budget so when you take the plunge you're doing it with your eyes open.

5. **We looked at how to discover what you can sell and to whom.**

   We looked in-depth at online networking, harnessing LinkedIn as a tool, utilising your network, and growing it one post, one comment, one message and one conversation at a time.

   We went through how important networking is and how it's not actually all that hard to do. We also underscored the value of just being a reasonable, helpful human being—and capitalising on these most basic of traits—to not be a dick and win business both now and in the future.

6. **Finally, we came back to the main ways of going it alone.**

   We went through being a service provider to individuals or businesses, day-rate contracting, passive income products, and the fact that no single way of working has to be mutually exclusive. Mix it up. Make it up. It's what everyone else is doing.

THE STORY

My mum said to me the other day:

"Where did we get the idea that when we become adults, we have to be able to do everything ourselves?"

It got me thinking. When we're children, we're learning all the time. Doing new things constantly. Right from birth, literally everything we do, we do for the first time. We teach our children to become more independent and able to do things for themselves. Along with making lots of mistakes, it's part of how we grow. Right through to when we're putting together those flat-pack wardrobes—sure, we might have learned how to use a screwdriver by then, but the instructions and the bits are new to us, so the first one always takes longer than the rest.

Kids (and their parents) have a greater choice of activities today than ever in our history. The breadth is staggering. They can choose what to learn at school, they can choose focused clubs (my son loves pottery club, and my daughter, after-school art). They can literally do a different thing every night of the week and more besides, plus cricket, football, rugby, netball, cross country, badminton or whatever to fill the weekend.

Yet, when we start *adulting*, focus can instead turn to going out and having fun, hobbies, travel and exploring new cultures, getting laid, drinking, building new friendships and relationships, establishing careers—and we think this is living an independent life.

And then, we normally stop.

Because we're focusing so much on the things we think we want to do with our lives (like making a living), we forget to build a life that's actually fulfilling. And sure, you might get tonnes of fulfilment from your job, but there is more to life than that. Surely?

I think that's why you've read this book.

And the longer we spend not learning how to do things, or leaving behind that thing we always wanted to do, the less likely we are to just pick something new up and have a go at it regardless of the outcome. You know, just for fun.

But it doesn't fit with our narrative. "I'm not the sort of person who [does *x*], so why would I even try it?" Well hold on, why would you be thinking about it if you didn't want to be the sort of person who does?

This is an example of the bullshit stories we tell ourselves. The ones that let us off the hook from trying something that we know is going to be hard work.

Have another think right now.

What's the one thing you dream of being able to do? Go on, what is it? Is it to travel solo across Europe? Is it to stand up in front of a crowd singing or playing an instrument, telling jokes, or performing your spoken-word poetry? Is it to share your days with the love of your life (who doesn't yet know that they are)? Is it to do a skydive? Or to go for that job? Is it to wear that amazing gold lame jumpsuit whilst playing guitar for a living and skydiving to the pub?

One of my clients recently listed seven things to answer the question "What do you want?", before saying "and probably get a job I enjoy".

I don't know, it's your question and your answer.

Now the important follow up question: "Why is it important to me?"

This is the key to breaking through, so hold on to that. You'll need to not only remember this, but live and breathe it when it gets tough. And it will.

The good news is there's specialist help out there for nearly everything. A coach for every situation. If you don't like the word coach, think of a teacher. Or a thinking partner. Someone who knows more than you about the subject, who's already done the hard yards so they can help you get on more quickly and avoid the pitfalls. Someone who has your back and wants to see you succeed. Or someone who can coach you through creating a vision and building the strategy, mindset, and capability to realise it. And keep you accountable. Someone like me. Me, in fact.

When we're young we have the ballet teacher. The piano teacher. The netball coach. The music teacher. If we're lucky, we have parents to guide us and help us grow, stretching us to achieve things we hadn't thought possible five minutes before.

They were there to give you the skills and confidence to try new things and become more skilled or capable.

And when you're coached and become practiced, you gain independence in doing it. But independence doesn't have to mean "Now I'm proficient I can never ask for help again", does it? Remember, every day's a school day.

Hugely successful businesspeople usually have a team of people around them to help them become even better. An executive assistant. A mentor. A coach. A therapist.

Elite sportspeople don't hit the big leagues and suddenly stop needing help. If anything they need more help—more help in accessing hidden parts of their physical and mental performance. They also pursue other completely different sports and get training in those too.

Men in particular are notorious for not asking for directions, ignoring instructions, and for thinking they don't need help. Why, I wonder?

I mean, I guess it doesn't matter why, but what's all the pig-headedness about? Is it a fierce protection of independence? "I don't need help, I've got this covered!" Does it go back to ancient ancestors hunting (or gathering) solo, where the only protection they had from a sabre-toothed tiger was a flint-fashioned spear and the ability to run? I don't know, but it just doesn't make sense.

Asking people to help you get to the place you want to get to more quickly—why might that be considered a sign of weakness, or somehow 'cheating'? And why is the pursuit of independence often seen as a solo one?

Maybe because to say we're not very good at something, to voice our dreams, or to tell people about our inner fears, is hard. It's being vulnerable. So it's easier to either just bulldoze your way through it and hope for the best, or do nothing at all (and grow old regretting not at least having a go).

Go back to the thing or things you really want to do. What if I told you that the things we desire most are often what we are most afraid of working on?

The things we desire most are often what we are most afraid of working on.

What if I muck it up? What if I embarrass myself? What if trying to do it means I have show up with vulnerability?

Well, what if it's easier than you thought, once you've taken a small step? How about putting on your big pants and braving it, like you did as a kid?

Do kids feel so much of this vulnerability? Perhaps some do, for some activities, and that's fine. But mostly they know no different and are less aware of the risks of embarrassment and losing face, so they just get on with it and get shown what to do, and get better and better at it whilst having their comfort zones gently stretched by their tutor. They'll fall over, sure, but they'll get up again. And have fun trying.

Ever seen a line of 20 five-year-olds snaking their way down a snowy mountainside on skis following a skiing instructor? I have, and it's a thing of innocence and fearlessness. Compare that with an adult clipping on skis for the first time. They're full of fear.

Five-year-olds also have less distance to fall. Both physically and mentally. Be more five-year-old.

What's the difference between a teacher of children and a teacher of adults?

Nothing. The difference is in the willingness of the student to stretch themselves and their belief in what they're capable of, whilst mentally reducing the distance they have to fall if they get it wrong—or doing enough of the hard prep work to reduce the risk of the fall in the first place. Or just getting comfortable with feeling uncomfortable.

So, what's the big thing you want to do that you've told yourself you can't?

And why is it important to you?

What happens if you *don't* take a step? How will you feel in five years?

What's the smallest step you can take to prove yourself wrong?

DECIDE IF YOU WANT HELP, OR IF YOU WANT TO GO IT ALONE IN GOING IT ALONE

I'd love nothing more than for you to take the contents of this book and crack on in making your mark on the world.

Whatever your choice please, please just start. Take the smallest step. Come on. You owe it to yourself.

And if you do want some help, get in touch and we can have a chat about what you want to achieve. No strings. **Just scan the QR code on the next page and get in touch.**

I'm great at this, and my clients come back to me time and again, like yours will. I'd love to help you realise your dreams.

Enough is enough.

NOW GO!

SCAN TO GET IN TOUCH WITH PHIL.

CHAPTER 19

30 TIPS WE WISHED WE'D HAD BEFORE WE STARTED

I asked some of my 'colleagues'—that is people in my network I trust, who have also made the shift to self-employment—what they wish they'd have known before they made the leap. Along with my own input, here's 30 tips, bits of advice, and real-life learnings for you.

1. Just because you have great accumulated knowledge, don't assume people will find you. Network. Post authoritative and problem-solving content on LinkedIn. Get recommendations and testimonials.

2. Put yourself out there, properly. Applying for contracts and talking to recruiters is not enough. Make a name for yourself in your market, in person, and on social media. Provide value and be authentically you.

3. Keep in touch with your network. And if you've lost touch, put yourself back in touch. Have an update call, find out what people are doing. And tell them what you're up to.

4. Niche. You don't have to focus completely on one type of person doing a particular job when thinking about who your clients might be. Think about the type of people you'd like to serve (like, how they think, rather than what they do), or the types of company, or the types of problems you solve.

5. If you try to be all things to all people, you won't be able to command as much authority as if you have a degree of specialism.
6. I could have done with a coach. Someone to challenge me and my thinking and give me support.
7. Avoid building up barriers to getting started. Setting up a company on the Companies House website really does just take two minutes and it's just a few quid. It'll take you longer to come up with a company name that isn't already taken.
8. Setting up a business bank account is quicker than you think. You only need your company name, company number (from Companies House), and some ID. Many banks are online-only and you can use their app to set it all up in a few minutes.
9. You don't need a finance app. You can create invoices in a Word template and keep track of them in an Excel spreadsheet. It doesn't need to be hard.
10. Not all contracts (long-term or otherwise) are advertised or given to a recruiter. You need to use your network or build one. Arrange virtual coffee chats. Lots of them. Find and create work. Ask people what their biggest challenge is. Offer to give them half an hour or an hour to talk it through. Give them some ideas. At the end of the call ask them if they'd be interested to know what doing that more regularly would look like.
11. Be prepared to agree to a lower rate for a bigger/longer-term piece of work and ask for a higher rate if it's a short piece of work.
12. Everything will feel uncomfortable. Get comfortable with feeling uncomfortable. It's the new normal.
13. Have a go. You won't know what it's like unless you do.
14. You don't need to have everything perfectly formed. Just start with what you have. Don't use a perceived lack of gear as an excuse to not start.

15. If you're going to promote yourself online, be quite explicit about what problems you solve and for whom.

16. It's never too late. I was 52 when I finally stepped out on my own. Age can be a benefit in contracting due to the volume of experience and expertise you've gathered in solving problems.

17. When people are telling you that you should go out on your own, that's the universe giving you permission. Listen to them, not your destructive self-talk.

18. Find your confidantes. People who have gone it alone. Contractors in your businesses. Connect with people on LinkedIn—tell them what you're doing and ask if you can pick their brains or buy them a coffee? Learn from them.

19. Enjoy the journey. It'll be hard, frequently. But there's a lot of reward available. Don't feel like you've got to go from 0-60 in three seconds. It's not a race.

20. Build a network—connect on LinkedIn with people you meet in each contract. Help them while you're working with them. Be a great colleague. Deliver. These are the people that might give you your future contracts or refer you to them.

21. You say you have no experience. What about all the years doing what you've been doing? All that experience gives you more than you give yourself credit for. How can you use all the non-subject-specific skills you've gathered?

22. You'll never reach a goal that you haven't defined. You might as well not have one. American author and motivational speaker Zig Ziglar told a story once about a guy at an archery range. In the story, they blindfolded the guy. "How can I hit a target I cannot see?" he said. Then, they took the target away altogether. "How can I hit a target that's not even there?".

23. Start smaller than you think.
24. Once you've created a vision it'll be easier to visualise and then work out the person you need to be in order to live in it...
25. ...and what those tiny steps or actions are that you can take today. It could be writing a post on LinkedIn or creating a new Instagram account, or combatting the fear of navigating a train station.
26. "Going it alone" doesn't mean you have to do everything yourself or actually be on your own. Build an informal team of people around you. People who have been there and are a few steps ahead. People who can recommend good accountants. People who help you feel like you're not alone.
27. Don't try to do everything at once. Do one thing differently for three months and see what the results are. Then tweak/add. Fail fast. Learn what works with minimal risk.
28. Find the sweet spot between the things you enjoy, the things the world needs, the things people will pay for, and the things you are good at.
29. Just do something. Then follow that with another something. Build momentum. Small steps will help you become more confident. With each step, you'll erode the fear and become braver to take the next one.
30. If you're struggling with motivation because of procrastination or one of the many other reasons I've cited so far in this book, think about this: motivation comes once you've started.

BONUS:

31. YOU ARE ENOUGH.

RESOURCES.

If you've enjoyed this book and/or found it useful (I honestly don't mind which, but hope for at least one) you might be wondering how you can get more ideas, support, or tools to help you make progress.

Well, you're in luck. **Scan this QR code** for further content from me that at the time of writing I either hadn't come up with, or didn't think would work so well in printed form.

SCAN FOR EXTRA RESOURCES
AND CONTENT.

ABOUT THE AUTHOR.

Phil Sterne first went out his own in 2014 after a 17-year career in recruitment, realising there was more to life than working in a company. Thanks to his wife Nicola giving him the nudge to seemingly risk everything and go out on his own, Phil started a whole new journey of self-employment. Her faith that he could make it a success and still pay the mortgage was incredible.

Since then, he's worked with leaders in just about every industry, supporting them in making life-changing decisions. Coaching them to help them understand their skills and capabilities, dreams and goals, barriers and blockers—and then helping them with the tools and confidence to take the next step.

He made just under £100,000 in his first year-and-a-half of going it alone, through a combination of gumption, audacity, and not being (too much of) a dick.

When he's not helping people live their most amazing lives, he reads thought-provoking non-fiction, watches thrillers, and enjoys walking in the Peaks and Lake District, riding his mountain bike in North Wales, and snowboarding in the Alps.

Phil's a dad to a daughter and a son. Family time is important, whether it's snowboarding, cricket, or art with his daughter, crafting and woodwork with his son, enjoying tasty meals and country walks with his wife, or just slobbing out together watching Deadpool.

Having the flexibility, time, and financial resources to do more of what he loves, whilst building a business and serving his clients powerfully is an ongoing challenge. But it's the choice he's made, and it's one of the best he's ever made.

If you'd like to book Phil for a 1-1 consultation, a corporate engagement, podcast or video appearances, interviews, or speaking, please **scan the QR code below** for details.

SCAN TO MAKE AN ENQUIRY.

THE ONLY
THING GETTING
IN YOUR WAY
IS YOU.

ACKNOWLEDGMENTS.

My wife, Nic, gave me the initial energy to go it alone. Without that, and the "It'll be alright" approach we took together, I wouldn't have done it. And I wouldn't have written this book. Thank you Nic for your encouragement and belief.

When I set out to write this book, I was a little confused about who I was writing it for. The lens that 'write it for one person' gave me was golden. I thank my coach, Adam Hulme, for bringing those words to my attention.

I immediately knew who I needed to write it for—me! Since realising the book needed to contain the advice and guidance I'd have found useful in those early days, it virtually wrote itself. Adam gave me the encouragement and focus to get going and promoted the discipline I needed to get through the writing process when it got tough.

As writing went on, I enlisted several friends and colleagues who had taken the plunge into self-employment as confidants and sources of inspiration for content. Dot Day, Stuart Robinson, June Hogan, and Debbie Sidwell provided me with their rich stories that helped inform my writing—thank you.

Couple that with the input from my early readers, Dave Scott, Pete McAllister, Si Gibson, Rachel Collier, Salma Craig, and Lorna Moles. Your feedback and success stories helped me tweak and tighten everything up, and gave me new ideas to help it serve my readers better. You also kept me focused on jumping the last few hurdles to get this published. Thanks to you and the many more people who volunteered.

Jo Everill and Quentin Lillis are up next. Central to helping me through the toughest period of poor mental health in my life, they helped me climb down from the bucking horse that was corporate life, and provided me with the human resources advice and guidance, coaching, and support I needed. Thank you both for helping me build the strength to go out on my own a second time.

Antony, my brother. We've had so many laughs at ridiculous scrapes we've found ourselves in over the years that are worthy of committing to a book. I'm just amazed that book didn't come out before this one. Maybe in the future? Thank you for always inspiring me to find new and interesting ways to encourage my creativity and to live well. And crucially for helping me get the final edit of this book over the line!

I can't write this without thanking my parents Julia and Ken for bringing me up with good morals, a caring nature, and a sound work ethic, and for the safety, love, and guidance they gave and continue to give me. They helped shape my values and my desire to help others lead better lives—which led to the writing of this book.

Dad: Thank you for helping me to improve my writing as a child and for encouraging me to set high standards for myself. Mum: Thank you for always inspiring me to follow my heart and do the right thing. I know you're both as proud of me as I am of myself for creating this work. And thanks to both of you for the inspiration I take from your unique life and career experiences, and your dreams (both met and not yet met)—they help me strive to live as close to my own 'best life' as I can.

And finally to you, reading this book. Whether you bought it or received it as a gift, thank you for picking it up. Now take the action: use the contents to build self-belief and go it alone.

I DARE YOU.

—PHIL

Printed in Great Britain
by Amazon

48777560R00128